ISBN 978-1-334-07498-1
PIBN 10708726

This book is a reproduction of an important historical work. Forgotten Books uses
state-of-the-art technology to digitally reconstruct the work, preserving the original format
whilst repairing imperfections present in the aged copy. In rare cases, an imperfection in
the original, such as a blemish or missing page, may be replicated in our edition. We do,
however, repair the vast majority of imperfections successfully; any imperfections that
remain are intentionally left to preserve the state of such historical works.

1 MONTH OF
FREE
READING

at
www.ForgottenBooks.com

By purchasing this book you are eligible for one month membership to ForgottenBooks.com, giving you unlimited access to our entire collection of over 1,000,000 titles via our web site and mobile apps.

To claim your free month visit: www.forgottenbooks.com/free708726

4488

HISTORY OF THE

POMEROY FAMILY

FROM 1572 TO 1880.

1572 - 1880

BY JOHN M. POMEROY,

EDITOR OF THE FRANKLIN REPOSITORY.

CHAMBERSBURG, PENN'A:
JOHN M. POMEROY, PUBLISHER.
1879.

INTRODUCTION.

I have seen it stated somewhere that almost any one who would go at the work with a determination to succeed, could trace the history of his ancestry for at least five generations with tolerable accuracy; and the statement will be borne out by the results. There is no difficulty in reaching back to our grandfather, for if he was dead before we reached the years of maturity, his children, or other of our relations who were contemporaneous with him, can tell us of his personal appearance, his manners, habits and peculiarities generally. But when we try to hear something of his ancestors, when their history is unwritten, and when we must rely upon tradition exclusively, the difficulty thickens, and we are content by getting the merest glimpses of their career, or an unimportant incident in their life. Even this is difficult to accomplish, as all who lived with them have also passed away. If there were some record kept in every family, some sketch however brief and imperfect of the different members composing it, the task to succeeding generations would be less difficult and much more satisfactory in its accomplishment. Young people, I have noticed, rarely feel much interest in tracing their family connections and history. It is only when the evening shadows begin to appear that they feel like trying to trace the long line of ancestry which has preceded them; how, where and when they lived, and when they died. It is sometimes unfortunate that this should be the case, as sources of information which are available at one period of our lives cannot be reached at another

The writer, when a boy, often listened to tales of the Revolutionary and Indian wars from Francis Graham, Jr., of Roxbury, a brother of our great grandmother, in which wars he participated, and for which services he was a pensioner of the United States, but I was then too verdant to know that he could give me valuable information in regard to our ancestors which I have recently exhausted myself unsuccessfully to procure.

In a purely Republican form of government like ours, where the law recognizes no distinction of persons and families, where there are no hereditary titles or estates, the family history is not so important as it is in monarchial countries, where important property interests are dependent upon it; still it is gratifying to see that as education advances and becomes more general, there is more attention paid to family history. And as our free institutions place the highest position within the reach of the humblest citizen, no one need be ashamed of his ancestry. If, as has been said, few of us could trace our ancestry back for five generations, without running against some grandfather who was a broken-backed shoemaker, coal heaver or beggar, let us congratulate ourselves that there was sufficient vitality in the blood which courses in our veins to rise to a higher and more influential position in life. As these sketches are intended for private, and not for general circulation, let not the facts of history be perverted, however, by implying from the above statement that I did in my searches unearth the characters described, but that, on the contrary, as the following pages will show, our ancestors never occupied any position in life below the middle or substantial class of people, while some were eminent in their several relations. Nor have I been able to find any public stain resting upon any of them. While they do not appear, except in a few instances, to have been possessed of great wealth, they have always, if poor, been respectable. A member of the family in Kentucky writes me that it was always a proud boast of her father, Isaac Pomeroy, a native of Franklin county, "that all the men in the family from the old French teacher down, had the reputation of being honest men, while all the women were chaste."   J. M. P.

THOMAS POMEROY.

THE FOREIGNER AND FIRST SETTLER.

***

CHAPTER I.

The Pomeroy family are of French origin. The name signifies "Royal Apple." Through successive generations the stock has become so impregnated with the Scotch-Irish, that the original blood has nearly disappeared, and there is little of the Huguenot left to us except the name. Descended as we are from these two races of people, we have a right to be proud of the ancestry from which we spring. In the days of religious persecution they were the bulwarks of Protestantism in Scotland, Ireland and France, and thousands of them met death in its most revolting forms in defense of their religious convictions.

The most remote ancestor to whom our branch of the family trace their origin, was a classical teacher who was employed as a tutor in the family of a French nobleman in Paris, at the time of the Massacre of St. Bartholomew, in August, 1572. His education and position must have made him a man of some importance at the gay capital of France among the Protestants, as he was a marked man by the Roman Catholics. A daughter of the nobleman in whose family he was teaching, and who may have been a Roman Catholic, conveyed to Pomeroy, for whom she had formed a strong attachment, intelligence of his dangerous position, and succeeded in getting him to the sea shore, where he went on board of a fishing vessel bound for Ireland, where he landed in safety. The lady who had thus

been instrumental in saving his life, joined him in time in Ireland, and they were married. They were entirely without means, and they supported themselves by teaching. Some of the descendents of this couple located in Liverpool, England, where they became merchants and dealers of different grades. A connected list of the descendents of the French teacher has not been preserved, or at least cannot now be found, and hence we cannot trace his genealogy perfectly to the present generation. But we know something of the history of Thomas Pomeroy, the first, who was his descendant according to his own testimony, in Europe, and know more about the latter part of his life in America. He was a merchant of moderate business and means in Liverpool. The circumstances of his leaving England for this country, as detailed by himself, were these: After closing his store one evening he was out on the street at a very late hour with some of his companions, who were all in a hilarious mood from the effects of a little too much liquor, when he was seized by a "press gang" who were forcibly drumming up recruits for the British Navy. England was at war at the time and was aspiring to be master of the ocean, as indeed she was, and for the great number of ships of war she had afloat, she had no adequate supply of seamen, and to obviate this difficulty she inaugurated a system of impressment into the Navy, which always caused uneasiness and terror throughout the kingdom. She enforced this cruel and arbitrary system for a century or longer, and even claimed the right to search the vessels of other nations for seamen whom she alleged had deserted from her Navy. It was the enforcement of this demand against one of the national vessels of the United States that culminated in our war with Great Britian in 1812. Although England does not now insist on this right, she never formally yielded it.

Thomas Pomeroy doubtless shocked by finding himself, much against his will, and contrary to all his business arrangements, an enlisted man in the British Navy, appears to have become suddenly sobered by the surprise and capture, and asked his

captors to accompany him to his store, where he determined to play the agreeable to them, and try if possible to make his escape from his embarrassing and uncomfortable position. When, at length, he succeeded in getting them to imbibe sufficiently to put them soundly asleep, and got the last man put away under the counter, he provided himself with Seventy Pounds Sterling in cash, and with this he went on board of a merchant vessel lying in the harbor, and bound for America, on which he had previously shipped some goods to this Country. He had a letter conveyed to his partner advising him of his adventure, and in a few hours the ship left the port of Liverpool, and he was moderately safe from a life he appears to have dreaded. From the fact that he was shipping goods, and had been trading somewhat with this Country, it is possible that he contemplated an early removal hither, and the event was only hastened by his misfortune on the night in question. The means he employed for his escape, and the presence of mind he displayed in the emergency, show that he was a shrewd man, and capable of surmounting serious difficulties when thrown in his pathway.

Arriving in America, which was then and for half a century thereafter, a colony of Great Britain, visions of the British Navy, and his possible arrest as a constructive deserter, appear to have disturbed his mind, and it is said he determined to locate where neither officers of the army or navy would be likely to encounter him. He apprehended that his name would be returned to the government as one who had been regularly impressed into the service, and had made his escape before being formally placed on duty, and knowing how relentlessly the impressment system was enforced against delinquents, he determined, if possible, to find a place of security. Hence he locatcated in what must then have been a wilderness, near the North Mountain, and near where the village of Roxbury was subsequently built. He changed his business and became a farmer, instead of a merchant as he was in Liverpool. It is quite probable that he changed the orthography of the name to Pumroy, in which way it was spelled until 1856. It was spelled

Pomeroy by the family in Europe, and by all the branches of the family in America, and never was spelled in any other way by any portion of the family, except ours. He may have wished to disguise his name in his secluded retreat. There is no evidence of this, and it is only conjectured. It may be as well to state just here, that all the members of the family agreed in 1856 to restore the original mode of spelling. The branches of the family in Kentucky, Illinois and Western Pennsylvania had corrected the orthography prior to that date.

Thomas Pomeroy, the first, settled among the earliest white settlers of Lurgan township, about the year 1730. I have searched the records of the Land Office at Harrisburg to ascertain the date at which he first acquired title to his real estate, but found no record whatever there. He may either have held it by possession and location, or he may have purchased the right of another party. It is certain, from evidence I have found elsewhere, that at a very early date he owned a large body of land on what is now the road to Newburg, about two miles below Roxbury. At the time of his location there he could as easily have had lands in the limestone part of Cumberland Valley, which is now much more valuable than the farms North of the Conedogwinet creek, but the early settlers in the valley believed the slate land vas superior to the limestone part of it, besides being much better watered. Hence the first settlements are said to have been made along the North mountain. There appears to have been no marked event in the history of the first Thomas Pomeroy after his landing in America, or at least history and tradition have given us none. He appears to have pursued the even tenor of his way, quietly cultivating his farm, living at peace with his neighbors and fulfilling all the duties of a good citizen. He raised a large family, eight children, four of whom were sons, and four daughters, survived him. He died about 1770. I hoped to get the date of his death more accurately from the records of Cumberland County, which at that date embraced Lurgan township, but learned with regret that the Recorder's office at

Carlisle was destroyed by fire in 1776, together with its contents. I found there the account of Thomas Pomeroy who was the administrator of his mother, widow of the first Thomas, from which it appeared that she died in 1777. Her name was Margaret.

His sons were named Thomas, John, George and Samuel. His daughters' names I have not been able to get, but one was married to a Mr. Doyle and another to Mr. Duncan, both of whom lived and died in Pennsylvania. Thomas Pomeroy, his oldest son, remained on the old homestead, but the other sons went westward at an early date. John first located in Westmoreland county, Penn'a, where he became a very prominent citizen. He was Colonel of a regiment in one of the Indian Wars, and so distinguished himself that he was afterwards familiarly known as "the Indian Killer." The Hon. Edgar Cowan of Westmoreland County, Penn'a., when a member of the United States Senate, once asked me if I was a member of the same family of Col. John Pomeroy. Replying in the affirmative, he told me that tradition said he wielded great power among the early settlers of that region, and that there is a district of Country in Westmoreland County where he lived that is still known as "Pomeroy's Plains." Acting as a magistrate, so great was the confidence of the people in his judgment and integrity, that nearly all unsettled business or other difficulties between neighbors, was referred to him for adjudication. As considerable crowds were sometimes present he would dispense justice under a large oak tree near his primitive cabin. The descendants of Col John Pomeroy reside mainly in Lawrence and Mercer Counties, Penn'a. Judge Thomas Pomeroy of Lawrence County served two years in the Pennsylvania Legislature, with the writer in 1846 and '47. George A. K. (Apple King as he was called), removed to Jefferson County, Kentucky, where he died. His descendants are scattered over Kentucky and the West, and so are the descendants of Mrs. Doyle and Mrs. Duncan. Of the others I have no specific information, except of our immediate ancestor Thomas..

Col. John Pomeroy was married at Roxbury, Penn'a., to Hannah Graham, sister of Mary Graham, the second wife of his brother Thomas. They had four sons named Francis, John, George and Thomas, and two daughters named Margaret and Mary, the former married Charles Boyle and the latter James Gibson. Francis, George and Thomas removed from Westmoreland County, Penn'a., to the neighborhood of Wooster, Ohio, and subsequently removed from there to points further west. John removed to Mercer, now Lawrence County, Penn'a., where most of his descendants still reside. He had four sons named Thomas, William, John and Joseph. The first three are dead, Thomas having died near the close of the year 1878, and his widow a few months thereafter. After having served two years with the writer in the legislature of Pennsylvania, as stated in a preceding page, he was for fifteen years an Associate Judge of the County of Lawrence, and held other prominent public positions. He was a ruling elder in the Presbyterian church, and was justly held in the highest estimation by his fellow citizens. Rev. Joseph S. Pomeroy, the only surviving brother, is Pastor of the Presbyterian church at Fairview, Hancock County, West Virginia. John S. Pomeroy, son of Judge Thomas Pomeroy, was Prothonotary of Lawrence County, and was killed at the battle of Gettysburg, where his remains repose in the National Cemetery, properly marked.

It is quite clear that the lands in Lurgan township were occupied many years by the first settlers under a sort of pre-emption title, and that warrants were issued, and surveys made upon them at a much later date. Thomas Pomeroy had a tract of 117 acres 95 perches surveyed on warrant December 17th, 1767. Another tract was surveyed to him on warrant in right of James M'Cormick, containing 160 acres 102 perches on the same day. On October 14th, 1775, another tract was surveyed to him on warrant containing 176 acres and 22 perches. A tract in Letterkenny township surveyed on warrant granted to John Pomeroy, May 20th, 1768, containing 24 acres, lying along the Conedogwinit creek, was held by him on an improvement right began

in 1736, and interest was charged him from that date. Doubtless the other tracts were held by improvement rights for many years. Francis Graham, Sr., the father-in-law of both Thomas and Col. John Pomeroy, lifted his warrant for 363 acres on the 8th of September, 1755. This is the farm adjoining Roxbury, the greater part of which now belongs to the great-great grandson of the first settler, Alexander W. Pomeroy.

The information as to the different warrants for land in Lurgan township was procured at the office of the Surveyor of Franklin County. It must also appear at the land office at Harrisburg, but my searches there were confined to an earlier date.

CHAPTER II.

THOMAS POMEROY THE SECOND.

The preceding contains all the information that we have been able to collect in relation to our original ancestor in this country, Thomas Pomeroy. And although meagre in its details, it has cost much time and effort to procure. Information that was sought, and on which much labor was spent, does not appear. For instance, I have entirely failed to ascertain who Margaret, the wife of the first Thomas Pomeroy, was, and I have been equally unsuccessful in fixing the family connection of the first wife of Thomas Pomeroy the second, who, with her two children, was murdered by the Indians. Other points of information may suggest themselves which the reader would like to hear, but they may be dismissed as not attainable. The author sought information for several years, and only when satisfied that I could get nothing more did I commit to paper, in a formal manner, what I had. That what we have is authentic, as far as it goes, there is no question, as the circumstances attending the removal of the first Thomas Pomeroy to America were stated by him to his children and grandchildren, and by them to their children, quite a number of whom are yet living. Other facts in regard to their places of residence, location of farms, &c., were derived from the records, and from the testimony of members of the fourth generation who were born at the ancestral home, the father of the writer and his brothers and sisters. The history of our remote ancestor, the Hugenot and teacher, was derived from Thomas Pomeroy the first, and is no doubt authentic.

There is a numerous family of our name in New York and New England, and throughout the West, who have a popular impression among them that all of the name in the United States are descended from Eltweed Pomeroy, who landed in Massachusetts from England about 1632. Recent correspondence with some of these parties developes the fact that they have not all sprung from that stem, and although some of our family have been inclined to believe that Thomas Pomeroy had emigrated from New England, and that he was consequently connected with them, I have satisfied myself by an examination of their family records that this could not be the case, before getting the clearest information that he was a foreigner. As the ancestor of the New England family, who was a gunsmith, came to this country the century after the massacre of St. Bartholomew, and consequently when the French teacher had many descendants in Great Britain, it is by no means improbable that Eltweed Pomeroy was one of them, and that we may thus all have a common father in the Parisian linguist. There are good reasons for supposing that this may be the case, the most prominent of which is the striking resemblance which some of the members of the New England family, whom I have seen, bear to their Pennsylvania namesakes. Some twenty years ago, when my mind first began to turn to the investigation of the genealogy of the family, I was introduced to Dr. Brownson in Philadelphia, a well-known literary character, who was somewhat famous for having renounced Protestantism and embraced Popery, who was then publishing a monthly periodical in the interests of the Catholic church. He asked me in the course of conversation whether we were connected with the New England Pomeroys, and I replied that it was not clear that we were. "Well," said he, "I can give you a sign by which you will know whether you are or not. It is a peculiarity of the family, and I am intimately and extensively acquainted with it, that they grow up slender men until they are about the age of thirty, when they begin to expand, and they grow until they become large men." I told him that was the case with a

majority of our family in this State, and he said that while there were exceptions to the rule in New England, this was the rule. I have had this statement confirmed by members of the family in the East, and it is a very strong point in favor of its unity. There is a family in England of our name whose founder was ennobled by William the Conqueror, but as William invaded England before the massacre of St. Bartholomew, his descendants cannot be connected with us, unless remotely with those of the French teacher, who escaped from Paris long after the advent of William and his army in England. This party was Ralph de Pomeroy, a young Frenchman, and therefore possibly of the same family, who was on the staff of William the Conqueror, and so popular and useful had he made himself, that when the Normans conquered England the King gave him a large body of land, and conferred upon him a title of nobility. As he also emigrated from France, although under different circumstances from our ancestor, the theory is thus further strengthened that all of the name are branches of the main stem in that country. In a closing chapter we will give some further facts in the history of Ralph de Pomeroy.

(It will not be amiss to apologize here, in parenthesis, for the frequency with which the personal pronoun *I* is used. These sketches were written at first without any expectation of their being published. When I began to copy them for publication, I thought of using the third person, but as all the correspondence and investigations had been conducted by myself, I did not see how I could very well make the change, and keep the narrative clear and intelligible. I will not make any attempt at enlarging the history beyond what a fair recital of the facts will require, nor throw in fiction where only the reality is wanted, and confine the work to the narrowest limits consistent with a full understanding of the subject in hand. This much by way of explanation of the apparently egotistical style adopted.) .

Thomas Pomeroy, son of our foreign ancestor of the same name, was born on his father's farm below Roxbury in 1733, and died either on that or the adjoining farm, both of which he

owned, sometime between the 26th of July and the 9th of September 1803. I got these dates from his will, which was executed on the former date, and probated on the latter. I have failed to procure the exact date of birth and death in many instances, after having tried every possible source of information. Thomas Pomeroy, the second as he may be termed, spent all of his three score years and ten in Lurgan township, dying nearly if not exactly on the spot where he was born. Although ranking as a highly respectable citizen, he does not appear to have filled any public position of importance. Engaged in the peaceful pursuits of agriculture, he was exposed to the perils of frontier life, and was in common with the early settlers of Cumberland Valley, harassed by the incursions of bands of hostile Indians, which resulted in the massacre of his family, he alone escaping. After the defeat of Braddock, July 9th, 1755, the French and their savage allies, the Indians, made hostile raids into Cumberland Valley, and their massacres were of the most brutal and revolting character, sparing, in their bloody course, neither age, sex nor condition. These raids of the savages were repeated, with more or less ferocity, at different intervals, between 1755 and 1770.

In the month of July, 1763, the savages appeared along the North Mountain, and I have this account of the circumstances under which the massacre of Thomas Pomeroy's family was effected from his niece, Elizabeth Curry, formerly Graham, now residing in Illinois, she having, as she says, got it from her father, Francis Graham, the brother-in-law of Thomas Pomeroy: "Uncle Thomas arose early one morning and went a short distance from the house to try to shoot a deer, and while he was gone the Indians came to his house, and killed his wife and two children." These victims of savage cruelty were buried on their farm. A local history of the Indian troubles in Cumberland Valley at that time, thus refers to that occurrence: "Thomas Pomeroy and his wife, and a Mrs. Johnson, were surprised in a house between Shippensburg and the North Mountain, and left there for dead, but one of the

women when found showed signs of life, and was taken to Shippensburg, where she lived some hours in a miserable condition. She was scalped, one of her arms was broken, and her skull was fractured by the blow of a tomahawk. Within a few days fifty-four persons were killed by the Indians in that region. Houses, barns and crops were burned; and the whole Valley seemed to be enveloped in a general conflagration. The whole country west of Shippensburg was laid desolate, and Shippensburg and Carlisle became the barrier towns. Dwelling houses and stables were crowded with refugees who had lost horses and cattle and harvest, and were reduced from independence and happiness to beggary and despair. The streets were filled with people distracted by grief for their losses, and surrounded by disconsolate women and wailing children."

The woman referred to in this extract was probably Mrs. Johnson, as I think Mrs. Pomeroy and the two children were killed immediately. The Johnsons and Pomeroys lived on neighboring farms. Mrs. Curry gives another point in relation to Thomas Pomeroy, which is not without interest, as it shows that his descendants come by their corpulency honestly. It is this: "I have heard father say that he was so fat that he was a burden to himself. His shirt collar was half a yard wide."

In the year 1844 I happened to be at a political meeting in Carlisle, Penn'a, which was addressed by Gen. Samuel Alexander, an eminent lawyer of that place. The Whig candidate for President was Henry Clay, and for Governor, Gen. Joseph Markle, whose principal element of popularity was his record as a fighter against the Indians on the Western frontier. The contest, as all will remember who participated in it, was bitter and exciting. General Alexander spoke of the hardships and sufferings endured by the early settlers, not only on the Ohio frontier, where Markle operated against the Indians, but also in Cumberland Valley, and spoke of Thomas Pomeroy often calling at his father's house near Newville, when he, the Gen-

eral, was a boy, and frequently remaining over night when it was too late to get home from his visit to Carlisle, and how he entertained him with stories of Indian troubles, and the dangers to which the early settlers were exposed. He said the old man was always a welcome visitor at his father's house, and particularly so to him and the younger members of the family, who were always sure to be entertained with Indian stories if he could remain over night. He spoke of him as not only being a very genial man, but as an estimable and highly respectable citizen. I have often regretted that I did not make myself known to Gen. Alexander after the meeting, and learn additional facts from him, but as I have said before, I took less interest in family history in those days than I have done since. Gen. Alexander died soon afterwards.

Mary Graham, the second wife of Thomas Pomeroy, was born in Lurgan township, March 5th, 1747, and died in April, 1815, aged 68 years. As she was the mother of what has grown to be a large family, a sketch of her would be interesting and valuable, but I have been unable to procure any material, although I might have had much from her brother Francis Graham, if I had been less intent on his Indian and Revolutionary stories. She was fourteen years younger than her husband. The date of her marriage is not in the family records now available, but it was probably in 1768, when she was 21 years of age, her oldest child John having been born February 25th, 1769. If so, Thomas Pomeroy remained a widower over four years after the terrible tragedy which destroyed his first family, and was married the second time when about 35 years of age.

He raised a large family. How many children besides the two killed by the Indians, if any, died I have no means of knowing without the family record, but the following reached the years of maturity: John, Thomas, Joseph, George, Francis, Charles, James, Isaac, Mary married to Mr. Caldwell, Margaret married to Mr. Adams and Elizabeth married to Mr. John

White. All of these went west except John, Charles and Mrs. White. They first settled near Louisville, Kentucky, but some of them subsequently scattered into Illinois, and probably other states. They all left children except Thomas, the third, who was unmarried, and who died at New Orleans of Yellow fever. He was engaged in boating on the Ohio and Mississippi rivers. When yet a citizen of Lurgan township, he was several years collector of taxes, and his reports in the Commissioner's office, which I have examined, show that he was an excellent penman, and I should think a good scholar. He died young, and this is all we know about him. Joseph and Mrs. Caldwell resided in Illinois where they died, and both have descendants there and in Indiana. Francis left daughters but no sons. George left both sons and daughters. Charles remained in Pennsylvania and died near Roxbury probably about 1825. He left sons Thomas, John and Charles W., and daughters Margaret and Elizabeth, the latter married to Michael Gamble of Franklin county, who died in 1871, leaving several sons in Path Valley. Thomas died in Mercer county, Penn'a., and his widow and some of his children reside in Shippensburg, Penn'a. Mrs. Elizabeth White died about 1840. By her father's will it appears she was not married at the time of his death, in 1803, but was married soon thereafter, as her oldest child Samuel E. White was born in 1806, who married Nancy E. Bowers in 1838. He died in 1871. Ebenezer, her second son, removed to Ohio, where he is still living. Thomas Pomeroy White, the third son, died in Baltimore a few years ago. John White, another son, died at Mount Carrol, Illinois, two years ago. A daughter was married to J. Harvey Allen, and is now living near Fayetteville, Franklin county, Penn'a., and the other was married to John Gillan, of the same county, who has been dead a number of years.

I neglected to state in the proper place in the first chapter, that Margaret, the widow of the first Thomas Pomeroy, died at the residence of her son, Col John Pomeroy, in Letterkenny township. It is probable that after the death of her husband

she went to reside with her son John. The records of the
Courts of Cumberland County show that she died in Letterkenny township, and there is some other evidence indicating
that she lived there in her last years.

John Pomeroy, the remaining member, and the oldest of
Thomas Pomeroy's family, was born on the 25th of February,
1769, in Lurgan township; was married to Elizabeth Nevin on
the 12th of May, 1794, and died in 1818. He was trained to
the life of a farmer on his father's property. His education
was limited to the meagre advantages afforded by the inferior
common schools of that period, and embraced only the elements
of a common English education. His father gave him one of
his farms in that township, but he does not appear to have
been successful as a farmer, and he did not retain the property.
Subsequently he located on a farm belonging to his father-in-
law, in Southampton township, Franklin County, where he remained until his death, which occurred in Shippensburg at the
house of his brother-in-law, David Nevin. He has been described to me by persons who knew him as a man of good personal appearance, of genial manners, strict integrity and industrious habits; a good citizen and kind neighbor and friend.
He was captain of a military company in his neighborhood,
and appears to have been locally popular, although I have not
heard that he had any ambition for political preferment. He
and his forefathers were men of a quiet, retiring disposition,
who apparently had no taste for politics or public life, but
found their happiness in the home circle and in the quiet but
peaceful pursuits of agricultural life. His death occurred in
this way: Being in the habit of making trips to Baltimore with
his wagon, as nearly all the farmers of that day did in the winter season, with their own produce and that of others, he was
taken sick on his way home, left his wagon and was brought
to Shippensburg in a sleigh, but could not reach his home,
which was some four or five miles from Shippensburg. He
went to the house of David Nevin and died there. Elizabeth
Nevin Pomeroy, his wife, was born December 4th, 1771 and

died in 1826, aged 55 years. The children of John and Elizabeth Pomeroy—I give them in the order of their birth, which
I am not certain I have done in the previous families—were
Daniel Nevin, Mary, Thomas, Joseph, John Nevin and William
Reynolds, all of whom were born in Lurgan township except William Reynolds, who was born in Southampton township, Franklin
County, Penn'a. Of these we will give some account in the
next chapter. Of this generation we can give our own im-
pressions, as we were contemporaneous with them, except in
the case of the oldest, of whom we have only a faint recollec-
tion. We never looked upon the face of any member of the
preceding generation that we are aware of.

John Pomeroy, and his father and grandfather, were all
buried at Middle Spring. Members of two generations of
their descendants who have since passed away, have been laid
beside them in that rural burying ground, among the old oaks,
where they will calmly sleep until awakened by the trump of
the resurrection. These are Mary and Thomas Pomeroy, and
the children of the latter, making in all five generations whose
remains are there entombed. In the early interments at the
old burying ground at Middle Spring, tombstones were unknown, and through the lapse of time and the passing away of
successive generations, the graves have become unknown to
most of those now living, and this, I regret to say, is the case
with the first three generations of our family who are buried
there. Professor William M. Nevin, in his well known poem
on Middle Spring, thus refers to this fact:

"In this high burial ground, in that below.
No massive structure stands of sculptured stone;
No columned shaft, oft broke, that it might show ·
Youth's vigor downward all untimely thrown,
But humble slabs and headstones many strown,
Simply the names and years and worth avow
Of these here laid. 'Tis well. They covet none.
In life they were plain men of honest brow;
They sought no honors then, nor do they seek them now."

It is pleasant to reflect that five successive generations have
repaired on each Lord's day to Middle Spring to worship the

God of their fathers. One generation has descended to the tomb, but the next has followed in their footsteps and taken their places in the sanctuary. Churches have been demolished and others and better ones have been reared in their places; old and faithful pastors passed away, and their places were occupied by others, but still our ancestors were found occupying a place in this ancient congregation of God's people. The Huguenot blood which flowed in the veins of our earliest ancestor of whom we have any knowledge, has always displayed its influence in his descendants, by their firm adherence to Christianity, and almost uniformly to the Presbyterian order and faith.

A LURGAN TOWNSHIP TRAGEDY.

After the disastrous defeat of Braddock in the summer of 1755, the Western frontier of Pennsylvania was desolated by a savage horde which swept unchecked over its territory, marking its course by the murder of its inhabitants and the destruction of their homes, crops and herds. This period of distress and alarm was not terminated until the conclusion of a treaty of peace between France and England in 1762, by which the possessions of the former in the North-west, including the chain of French forts from Detroit to the Monongahela, fell into the hands of the English. The murderous inroads of the Indians, encouraged by the French, were temporarily interrupted by the withdrawal of the French soldiers, by whom these forts were garrisoned, and the substitution of British troops.

The Indians, who had quietly acquiesced in the building of these fortifications and their occupancy by their former allies, the French, although their title to the lands upon which they stood was not extinguished by purchase from their original owners, were not yet disposed to allow their transfer to their old and hated foes without an effort upon their part to prevent it. Consequently, the calm which now pervaded the Western

portion of the Province, was soon to be broken by a fiercer and more murderous irruption than it had previously suffered.

Early in the year 1763, the celebrated Ottawa Chief, Pontiac, made a most vigorous and well planned attempt to conquer these forts, lately fallen into the hands of the British, and also drive the white settlers, with the tomahawk, scalping knife and fire, from the hereditary possessions of the Red Man. A simultaneous and cunning assault was made upon the forts extending from the great lakes along the North-western border of the Province, reaching as far East as forts Ligonier and Bedford. Most of these works fell by strategy and their garrisons were cruelly murdered with all the brutal atrocity characteristic of savage warfare. While these assaults were being made by large bands of Indian warriors, the remoter settlers of Pennsylvania, west of the Susquehanna, were traversed by small parties of exasperated savages, whose unexpected visits to the devoted settlers were marked by death and desolation.

Franklin county, then included in Cumberland, suffered severely from these roving fiends incarnate, and those inhabitants who escaped were driven from burning houses and sought safety in Shippensburg, Carlisle and in the more distant towns beyond the river. Many houses in the vicinity of Rocky Spring, Strasburg and the adjacent country were burned and their occupants either killed or carried into captivity by the savages. During this terrible ordeal, large portions of the western division of the Province almost reverted to their original condition in consequence of their total depopulation.

These murdering marauders reached the settlements by crossing the Kittochtinny Mountain through the numerous gaps which provided natural highways. These passes were guarded to some extent by rude block houses and forts, which were defended by the inhabitants of the neighborhood and the several companies of rangers enlisted for the defence of the frontier. Among other posts of this description distributed along the foot of the mountain, and reaching nearly to the Potomac, was a

stockade fort at M'Allister's Gap, below which stands the town of Roxbury.

In the winter of 1764, this work was garrisoned by an "officer and 18 men," which fact is learned from a map of the period, showing the distribution of fortifications along the mountain foot in that year. Indian murders must have been comparatively infrequent in this vicinity, as history and tradition are equally silent in relation to them, if we admit a single exception. One reason for this immunity can doubtless be referred to the fact that the country in the neighborhood of Roxbury was at this early date very sparsely settled, and did not present to the prowling Indian as inviting a prospect for the gratification of his murderous propensities as were offered by the more numerous settlements in other directions.

Among the first of the pioneers who sought homes in this remote western wilderness, which was almost exclusively peopled by Europeans, chiefly the historic Scotch Irish, was Thomas Pomeroy. One of this gentleman's early ancestors was a French Huguenot, and, at the time of the massacre of Saint Bartholomew's day in 1572, was engaged in teaching school in Paris. On the night of that terrible tragedy, in company with some other Huguenots, he escaped to Ireland. Thomas Pomeroy, the first of the family who came to America, was born in Ireland, and removed to Liverpool in which town he was engaged in mercantile pursuits previous to his removal to America, early in the eighteenth century. Soon after his arrival he removed to Lurgan township, and settled in what was literally and unquestionably a howling wilderness. The location he selected was about two miles East of Roxbury, on a small stream which rises in the neighboring mountain, and is now known as Rebuck's Run. Here he began to clear away the dense forest, and soon had wrested sufficient space from the hand of Nature to afford him a site for his rough log cabin, with its huge stone chimney built on the outside, and a small additional patch to serve as a garden.

As time rolled on numerous children were born in the family,

one of whom bore his father's christian name of Thomas, which has been conferred upon different members of the family in successive generations. The elder Pomeroy died about the beginning of the Revolution, when his son Thomas, who was born in Lurgan township in 1733, had reached the years of mature manhood. All the children of the first Thomas Pomeroy, with the exception of his son Thomas, went further West and located in Westmoreland and Mercer counties, and some of whom become conspicuous in the subsequent wars with the Indians. Thomas, the second, settled near the ancestral cabin, where he also lived happily and prosperously with his increasing family, until the treacherous savage brought death and devastation to his devoted threshold. The cabin of Thomas Pomeroy at the time of the Indian hostilities during the conspiracy of Pontiac, was situated about a mile and a half from Roxbury, on the run previously indicated, on a gentle elevation which ascended from the stream　Here he lived a secluded and uneventful life, cultivating a small tract of land and devoting some of his leisure time in fishing and in the pursuit of the game which then abounded in the forest which surrounded his habitation.

His quiet and peaceful life was, however, soon to suffer a terrible and crushing interruption. The insidious and crafty Indian suddenly swept over the region along the base of the mountain, horribly massacring and mutilating its terror-stricken inhabitants, and visiting among many other cabins, the unsuspecting household of Thomas Pomeroy.

Early on the morning of July 21st, 1763, Thomas shouldered his rifle and proceeded to a "lick" or drinking place, not far from his dwelling, for the purpose of shooting a deer, as these graceful animals were accustomed to pay frequent visits to this locality.

Returning to his house after a short absence, a shocking scene presented itself to his terrified gaze. His wife and two children had been tomahawked and scalped by a small party of lurking Indians, who had doubtless concealed themselves in the vicinity until the family was left unprotected by its protector and head.

A Mrs. Johnson who was an inmate of the house at the time, was similarly treated, and left by the savages as dead. She, however, in the language of a contemporary publica ion the *Pennsylvania Gazette*, "showing some signs of life, was brought to Shippensburg, in a most miserable condition some hours afterwards being scalped, one of her arms broken, and her skull fractured with a tomahawk."

These unfortunate victims of savage ferocity were buried a short distance from the place of their murder, on a spot of ground, on which the barn belonging to the late John A. Rebuck, was subsequently built. This locality is on the State road, leading from Roxbury to Newburg, Cumberland county.

Thomas Pomeroy, in whose family the tragedy occurred, was the grandfather of the late Judge Thomas Pomeroy, of Roxbury, so widely known and esteemed in this section of his native State. Some years after the death of his wife, Thomas Pomeroy married a daughter of Francis Graham, Senior, who owned and lived on the farm adjoining Roxbury on the east, now owned by his descendant Alexander W. Pomeroy. He died in 1803, leaving a large landed estate in the vicinity of Roxbury."

W. C. L.

[The preceding article, written by Dr. William C. Lane, appeared in the *Franklin Repository*, January 21st, 1877.]

The will of Thomas Pomeroy, the second, will be found recorded in the Register's office of Franklin county, September 9th, 1803. It was executed on the 26th of July previous. From this it appears that he had made advancements of money to all his sons and daughters who had removed to the West, mostly to Kentucky, and bequeathed them an additional amount of cash in full of their respective shares. After making ample provision for his "dearly beloved wife Mary," by giving her part of the mansion house, well furnished, and a sufficient revenue from the farms bequeathed to his son Charles, he bequeaths the farm "on which my dwelling house and barn

are built, adjoining lands of John Pomeroy, Henry Reabuck and others, being part of the lands I now occupy, containing one hundred and sixty acres." He also gave to his son Charles a tract of land in Amberson's Valley containing one hundred and sixteen acres. He gave to his son James a tract of land containing one hundred and seventeen acres, adjoining the mansion farm, when he should arrive at the age of twenty-one years, in February. 1810. During his minority James was directed to live with his brother Charles, who was to have the proceeds of the farm, but was to supply James with "boarding and wearing apparel befitting a youth in his place and station," and when James reached the age of twenty-one, he was to give him certain live stock and farming implements, which he mentions particularly. He states that as "I have previously conveyed to my eldest son John the land whereon he now lives, I allow that to be in full of his share." The only bequest he made to any of his grandchildren was to Thomas, who was then two years old. He left him fifty pounds, which he directed to be kept at interest until he should arrive at the age of twenty-one years.

The will closed thus: "Further it is my will and desire that if any of these, my legatees, should bring forth, or cause to be brought forth, any dispute respecting this my estate, or this my last will and testament, (as I fondly hope there should be none), then in such case the parties thus disputing I allow to choose each a man to hear the complaint, and judge between them, but and if in case the said two men should not agree in their judgment, then I allow them (the said two men) to choose a third man, the judgment of which men shall be as binding on the parties, as though confirmed by any court of justice in the United States. And lastly, I nominate and appoint my trusty friends, John Maclay, Jr., (commonly known by name as Mountain John Maclay), Joseph M'Kinney and James Strain, all of Lurgan township aforesaid, executors of this, my last will and testament."

CHAPTER III.

Daniel Nevin Pomeroy, the oldest child of John and Elizabeth Nevin Pomeroy, was born in Lurgan township on the 8th of February, 1796, and died in Shippensburg on the 9th day of February, 1827, aged 31 years. He grew up on his father's farm, near Roxbury, and had the advantages only of a common school education, but from numerous letters and papers of his in my possession, including his account books, he would appear to have been a rapid penman, and quick and accurate in figures, possessing a fair business education. When quite young he began to learn the business of a tanner and currier. While serving his apprenticeship his father died, and his younger brothers being small, and the family not having been left in comfortable circumstances, it was necessary for him to return home, and with his younger brother, Thomas, conduct the operations of a farm which belonged to the estate of his grandfather, Daniel Nevin, upon which his mother and her family were mainly dependant for support. Whether after his mother subsequently removed to Shippensburg, he completed his apprenticeship, I am not advised; but he must have considered himself master of his trade, as he made it the business of his life. He was married on the 15th of January, 1822, to Jane Means, daughter of John Means of Shippensburg, Penn'a, who was also a tanner, and as I notice by his books that he was dealing in hides and leather at that place as early as 1820, it is probable that he rented the tan yard of Mr. Means two years before he was married to his daughter. Mr. Means died in 1823, a year memorable in Cumberland Valley as one in which a malignant fever prevailed that carried off large numbers of her citizens. The

tannery with a tract of land on the turnpike West of Shippensburg, and another tract in what is known as the "Pines" near
Shippensburg, became the property of my father and mother.
All this property was sold by myself and sister after we attained our majority. Daniel Nevin Pomeroy had two children,
John Means Pomeroy and Elizabeth Nevin Pomeroy. While
thus possessing through his wife a tannery and a house in a good
location, with well stocked tanyard which he was successfully
conducting, as well as the farming and timber lands of excellent
quality near his residence he was comfortably fixed, and every-
thing so far as outward appearances were concerned betokened
for him a successful career. But "man proposes and God dis-
poses," and in this case a hardy robust man, who never had any
serious sickness was cut off suddenly after an illness of only
about twenty-four hours. He was out at his woodlands at the
"Pines" and when he came home it was noticed that a small
pimple on his face looked red and angry, which soon developing
into a carbuncle with erysipelas tendencies put an end to his
existence. He was a member of the Presbyterian Church in
Shippensburg, was very highly esteemed in that community and
was a genial upright gentleman, with excellent social qualities
and fond of the company of his friends. As he died when the
writer of these sketches was only four years old my personal
recollections of him are very dim and indistinct. I can, however,
remember some incidents in connection with him, and remember
distinctly, his death and funeral. His weight is said not to have
exceeded one hundred and sixty pounds, but if he had lived
longer he would doubtless have been larger after the fashion of
the family.

His sister Mary and brother Joseph have often told me that
when he was young he was passionately fond of fishing, and
that when they lived on Herron's Branch he would very often
after a hard day's work in the harvest field go to the creek at
night to fish. His favorite way of fishing was with the gig,
and this required him to have some assistance in carrying the
light, which was made out of pine wood cut into splinters.

His brother Thomas, who was the largest and strongest of his younger brothers, generally performed this service for him, but sometimes he demurred, as he thought there was too much of it, and besides he said Nevin did all the giging while he had to carry the light.

Jane Means, his wife and my mother, was born Nov. 7th, 1804, and was married January 15th, 1822, when 17 years and 2 months old. Her father, John Means, was one of the most estimable of men, a ruling elder in the church at Shippensburg, and as an old citizen recently told me, "he lived in that community a life of peace, uprightness and great usefulness, and when he died he was greatly lamented by all the old as well as the young." Her mother was Mary Patterson, a sister of John Patterson, known as "Merchant John," of Juniata county, who died in 1836. As he was the grandfather of my wife, it follows that my mother and my wife's mother were first cousins. She died in 1826, and it is a singular coincidence that while her husband lived 60 years, 9 months and 12 days, she lived 60 years, 9 months and 11 days.

My mother died on the 1st of March, 1830, at the early age of twenty-five. This was three years after the death of my father, and when I had reached the age of seven years. I can remember her, not with sufficient distinctness to describe her, but I am told that she was rather more than of medium height, rather slender and quite good looking. She discharged all the duties of life faithfully, and passed early to her reward.

My father and mother were first buried in the yard attached to the old white Presbyterian church in Shippensburg, but about the year 1860 their remains were removed to Spring Hill Cemetery, at that place.

Daniel Nevin Pomeroy was called Nevin Pomeroy, the Daniel, except when his name was written, always having been omitted.

John Means Pomeroy, the only son of Daniel Nevin Pomeroy, was born in Shippensburg, April 1st, 1823. Soon after the death of his father, his mother being in delicate health, he

was placed in charge of his uncle Joseph at Concord, and he divided his time between him and his mother, until her death in 1830, after which he was at Concord all the time. When about twelve years of age he went into his uncle's store, and with some short intervals was engaged in mercantile pursuits until his purchase of the *Franklin Repository* in August, 1874. So far as education is concerned, he may be called a self made man, as the only training he ever had was in the common school at Concord, and a term of six months in an Academy at Chambersburg.

In October, 1845, he was elected on the Whig ticket a member of the Legislature from Franklin county, and was re-elected the following year. When residing in Philadelphia in 1859, he was elected a member of the Common Council, but declined a re-nomination and accepted instead an election as delegate to the Republican National Convention of 1860, where he supported the nomination of Abraham Lincoln. During the war he was for two years a Paymaster in the United States Army.

On December 9th, 1846, he was married to Rebecca C. Kelly of Juniata county, Penn'a. Her father, Col. William C, Kelly, was a well known citizen of that county of much personal popularity, and unusually attractive in his personal appearance. He died in 1829, before the birth of his daughter Rebecca.— His wife was Sallie Patterson, of Tuscarora Valley oldest daughter of John Patterson, merchant, who died about 1834. She has often been described as a most estimable and very superior woman. Four of their children lived to the years of maturity. John P. Kelly, the oldest, lives on his farm in Beale township, Juniata county. James Lyon Kelly studied medicine, and was practicing at Patterson, Juniata county, when he died at the age of about thirty years. Isabella Jane was married to J. Nevin Pomeroy, December 24th, 1867, and resides in the mansion house of her grandfather in Beale township, Juniata county. Rebecca, the youngest, is the wife of John M. Pomeroy as before stated.

John M. and Rebecca C. Pomeroy have been blessed with six children, four of whom died in childhood, the survivors being John H. and Albert Nevin. The record of Daniel Nevin Pomeroy and his children, and grandchildren, is as follows:

Daniel Nevin Pomeroy, born February 7th, 1796.

Jane Means Pomeroy, born November 7th, 1804.

Daniel Nevin Pomeroy and Jane Means married January 15th 1822.

John Means Pomeroy, born April 1st, 1823.

Elizabeth Nevin Pomeroy, born July 14th, 1825.

Daniel Nevin Pomeroy died February 8th, 1827.

Jane Means Pomeroy died March 1st, 1830.

John M. Pomeroy and Rebecca C. Kelly married December, 9th, 1846. Their children were born as follows:

Daniel Nevin, March 23d 1848.

Ellen Jane, October 4th, 1850.

William Kelly, June 13th, 1854.

John Heck, December 17th, 1856.

Albert Nevin, May 27th, 1859.

Sallie Bell, July 17th, 1862.

DEATHS.

Daniel Nevin, March 6th, 1853, aged nearly 5 years.

Ellen Jane, March 9th, 1853, aged about 2 years 5 months.

William Kelly, July 23d, 1862, aged over 8 years.

Sallie Bell, July 15th, 1871, aged 9 years.

At the present time (July, 1879), John H. and A. Nevin are engaged with their father in publishing the *Franklin Repository*, Chambersburg, Pa.

Elizabeth Nevin Pomeroy, the only daughter of Daniel N. Pomeroy, after the death of her parents was placed in the care of her aunt Mary, by whom she was reared. After the death of her aunt in 1857, she made her home in the family of her uncle Thomas, giving a large portion of her time to her brother's family, and this arrangement continues to the present time. At the age of about fifteen years, signs of deafness began to develop, which gradually grew worse until she became quite hard

of hearing. This is a family misfortune which has come from our ancestors. The great majority escape it, but some one in nearly every family is thus afflicted.

-- --

Mary Pomeroy, the only daughter of John and Elizabeth Pomeroy, was born in Largan township, October 23d, 1798, and died at Roxbury, same township, July 23d, 1857, aged 58 years and 9 months. Never having married, she lived with her mother until her death in 1826, when she went to Roxbury and kept house for her brother Thomas until his marriage, after which, for several years, she spent her time mainly with her brothers in Roxbury and Concord, until about the year 1839 when she opened house herself in Roxbury, and so continued until her death. She had charge of my sister after the death of our parents, and in 1836, upon the death of Julia Pomeroy, wife of John N. Pomeroy, she took charge of his children William F. and Julia A. Pomeroy. All these children she raised with a motherly care and tenderness, which did infinite credit to her head and heart; and the survivors of them have reason to be thankful to-day that in their orphanage they had a friend who was able and willing, and withal so well qualified to fill a mother's place. They owe her memory a lasting debt of gratitude. She was a woman of ardent temperament, of great firmness and determination in whatever she believed to be right, and devotedly attached to her relatives and friends. She was a member of the Middle Spring Church nearly all her life time, and was active in all good works, and she took for many years an active interest in sustaining a Sabbath School at Roxbury. She was not only a woman of decided convictions, but of strong common sense. Her death was very sudden. She had been suffering for several days with a sore leg, but was not supposed to be in any dangerous condition. Retiring to bed, and walking up stairs as usual with her two nieces, Elizabeth and Julia, who with herself constituted her family, she lay down on the bed, at midnight called to Julia, and immediately expired, apparently meeting a painless death.

Thomas Pomeroy, the third member of this family, and bearing the family name, was born near Roxbury on the 11th day of July, 1801, and died at Roxbury on the 13th day of January, 1871, aged nearly 70 years.

He was raised with his father on the farm and received, like the older children, only a limited common school education. Reference is made to the fact, in the sketch of his older brother, that they cultivated the farm after their father's death, and thus aided largely in the support of the family. At an early age he went to his uncle William Reynolds, Esq., to learn the trade of a tanner, and after serving the usual term of apprenticeship, he embarked in that business on his own account in Roxbury, on the property where he lived for nearly half a century, and where he died. This tannery was the gift of his granduncle, John Williamson, of Charleston, S. C., a bachelor of large wealth, who left him at his death some $5,000, in addition, and left nearly all the descendants of his sister, Mrs. Daniel Nevin, considerable sums of money, he being probably the wealthiest man our family has yet produced. Thomas Pomeroy after pursuing the tanning business for several years successfully, began to turn his attention also to merchandizing, and lumbering from extensive tracts of woodland which he had purchased in the North Mountain, and invested part of his gains in farms near Roxbury, which he judiciously purchased at very low prices, and which, at his death, had very largely enhanced in value. Of popular manners, of unbending integrity, of considerable energy of character, and ardently attached to the fortunes of the Whig party, he became prominent in their counsels, and was in 1844 elected to the office of County Commissioner, the duties of which responsible position he discharged for three years with zeal and fidelity, and in such a manner, as to increase his popularity, and bring him into wider notice and influence. In 1851 he was elected Associate Judge of Franklin county, which place he occupied with equal fidelity and satisfaction for five years. Thomas Pomeroy was about 5 feet 10 inches high and inclined to corpulency. He was a man of iron frame, and never suffered from sickness or ill health. A few days before

his death he complained of being unwell, but was attending to out of door business the day before his death. About six o'clock in the morning, while sitting in his arm chair near his bedside, he suddenly expired without giving any premonition of the sad event to his friends, none of whom were with him except his wife.

His children who survived him are Mary Jane, married to S. D. Herron; John Jay, Stephen Wilson, Alexander Wilson and William C. Those who preceded him to another, and we trust a better, world, were Elizabeth Nevin, Thomas, Andrew and Anna Elizabeth.

It is proper to say that Thomas Pomeroy, instead of courting political distinction, rather shrank from it. I was in the Convention of 1844 as a delegate when he was nominated for Commissioner, having just then attained my 21st year, and I was also present as a spectator in the Convention of 1851, when he was nominated for Judge, and in neither instance did he make the slightest effort to secure the nomination. They were entirely unsolicited, although the nominations at the time were considered equivalent to an election. He left an estate valued at some forty or fifty thousand dollars.

This brief sketch of the life of Thomas Pomeroy, who was a member of the fourth generation in Lurgan township, each preceding one having a Thomas, might be extended, but I find several points in his career so well put in an editorial of the *Franklin Repository*, January 25th, 1871, that I will adopt it in addition to what I have written:

OBITUARY.

"We announced last week the death of Judge Thomas Pomeroy, of Roxbury, the news of which reached us just as we were about putting the REPOSITORY to press. We present this week some further details of his life and the particulars of his death.

Judge Pomeroy was born in Lurgan township, near Roxbury, in 1801. At an early age he removed to Roxbury and commenced the business of tanning, at which he spent many years of his early manhood. At a later period, he also engaged in

mercantile pursuits, in which he continued to engage until his
sons were old enough to relieve him from the cares of the
store, when he relinquished business in their favor. He then
devoted all his time to the management of his several farms
and the superintendence of a steam saw mill, which he erected
in Roxbury about two years ago, and in the management of
which he continued until his death. He was of an active disposition and industrious temperament, and thoroughly managed his large and varied business, giving to every part of it
his constant personal supervision.

In 1850, when the judiciary was made elective by the people, he was elected one of the Associate Judges of the District.
He was also chosen County Commissioner and served with an
honest and intelligent zeal which was characteristic of the man.
Although frequently solicited by his friends to permit his name
to be used for various positions of trust within the gift of the
people, he invariably declined, as his tastes inclined him to the
less conspicuous though more congenial duties of domestic life.
The honors of the politician had few charms for him, and these
insufficient to withdraw him from the chosen path of his agricultural pursuits.

Judge Pomeroy entertained very decided political opinions,
and was an unwavering supporter of the Republican party and
its principles. Yet he was tolerant of political difference and
charitable in his judgment of those who believed and acted
differently from himself. As a neighbor and a friend, he was
the kindest of men; and his goodness of heart towards those
whose circumstances appealed to his generosity, is proverbial
in the community in which he lived the allotted three score
years and ten. No one can specify one single instance of
severity in the treatment of the large number of those whom
he befriended, and large pecuniary losses have doubtless been
the result of his indulgence to those who were under obliga-
tions to him.

Judge Pomeroy was a gentleman of fine presence, and of exceedingly courteous and pleasing manners, and readily accessible
to all who chose to appreciate him; yet, withal, possessed of a

quiet native dignity, which always commanded respect, and repelled rudeness.

His health was robust until within a comparatively recent date, when symptoms of heart disease began to present themselves, although they did not withdraw him from his usual busy daily pursuits. He died a sudden and painless death, while seated in his armchair, on Friday morning, January 13th, at about 6 o'clock.

His remains were buried at Middle Spring on the following Sunday, and notwithstanding the inclemency of the weather, were followed to the grave by a large number of his friends and neighbors, many of whom came from considerable distance to engage in this sad duty to our honored and cherished friend."

Thomas Pomeroy was married to Mary Ann Wilson, second daughter of Col. Stephen Wilson who resided near Roxbury, a very prominent citizen who represented Franklin county in the Legislature three years. She survives her husband, and we can only say of her living, as we would say of her if dead, that she is a most estimable, amiable and accomplished christian woman, of whom her children have just reason to be proud, and to pray that her life may be spared to them and her friends for many years.

The mother of Col. Stephen Wilson was a Porter, an aunt of David R. Porter, who was twice elected Governor of Pennsylvania. The late Gen. Porter Wilson, of Huntingdon, a full cousin of Mrs. Pomeroy, carried this part of the ancestral name. Col. Stephen Wilson was married to Mary Culbertson, daughter of Alexander Culbertson, who lived near Pleasant Hall, on the farm owned by the heirs of the late Solomon Cramer. She had six brothers all of whom made their home in or near Zanesville, Ohio. They were named Samuel, Alexander, William, James, Robert and John. She had two sisters, Elizabeth who was married to Jacob Cassel of Upper Strasburg, and Margaret who was married to Hon. William Maclay of Fannettsburg, Penn'a. Mr. Maclay was a member of the Legislature, Associate Judge and Member of Congress from Franklin county.

The father of Col. Stephen Wilson, was Andrew Wilson, of

Scotch-Irish descent, who came from Bucks county, Penn'a, to Letterkenny township.

The other children of Stephen and Mary Wilson were: Alexander, Elizabeth married to Davidson Herron, Sarah married to Rev. T. M. Sparks, Margaret married to William Herron, Andrew died unmarried, Caroline, married Henry Cane, Stephen Porter, died in infancy.

It is not the purpose of the author of this work to give any extended sketch of any of the representatives of the generation of which he is himself a member. The great object was to gather up what was yet available in the history of those who preceded us, and put it in permanent shape, so that those who will follow us can continue the narrative, and thus have a connected history of the family back at least to the sixteenth century. The book is intended only for the eyes of the members of the family now living, and their descendants. To our successors we can leave the work of doing justice to the memory of those now living, and they can fill up the sketches, the mere outlines of which are here given, and also bring up the history to a later period.

John Jay Pomeroy, the oldest son of Thomas Pomeroy, remained with his father in Roxbury until the spring of 1849, when he entered Tuscarora Academy, Juniata county, Penn'a, where he remained some time, and subsequently for some time was a clerk in stores at Academia and Port Royal. In 1852, at his own urgent request, he returned to Tuscarora Academy, and renewed his studies with a view of entering College. United with Middle Spring Church, April 20th, 1853. Entered Sophomore Class of Lafayette College, at Easton, Penn'a, in fall of 1854. Graduated July, 1857. Spent most of the year after leaving College teaching a private school near Rodney, Jefferson county, Mississippi. Entered Princeton Theological Seminary September, 1858. Graduated April, 1861. Was licensed to preach by the Carlisle Presbytery, April 10th, 1861, in Pine Street Church, Harrisburg, Penn'a. Ordained by the Presbytery of Lewes, in the Presbyterian Church, Dover, Del.,

November 28th, 1861. Was stated supply of Dover, Delaware Presbyterian Church from June 1st, 1861, to November 28th, 1861, and pastor of this church from November 28th, 1861, to October, 1862.

Was Chaplain of the 32d regiment Pennsylvania Volunteers, known as the 3d Regiment Pennsylvania Reserves, from October 12th, 1862, to June 17th, 1864, when the term of the regiment expired. Was Chaplain of the 198th Regiment Pennsylvania Volunteers from September 15th, 1864, to June 3d, 1865, close of the war. (See testimonial of officers of the 3d regiment Pennsylvania Reserves, and also acknowledgment of watch). Chaplain of the Military order of the Loyal Legion of the United States, in Philadelphia, from 1866 to 1877. Elected pastor of the Upper Octorara Presbyterian Church, in Chester county, Pa,. August 29th, 1865, installed November 14th, 1865, dissolved February 9th, 1875. Elected pastor of the First Presbyterian church, Rahway, N. J., January 5th, 1875, installed April 29th, 1875. Commissioner to the General Assembly of the Presbyterian church in 1870 at Philadelphia, in 1873 at Baltimore, Md., in 1879 at Saratoga Springs, N. Y. Delegate to the Presbyterian Convention in the interest of Church Union, meeting in Dr. Wylie's church, Philadelphia, November 6th, 1869. Delegate to the Evangelical Alliance in New York, October 2–12, 1873. Married January 28th, 1869, to Mary H. Moore, eldest daughter of Hon. Robert Moore of Danville, Pa. The Moore family were Presbyterians of Scotch-Irish descent. The family at an early day located near the north branch of the Susquehanna in the vicinity of Danville, Montour county. Mary H. Pomeroy's grandfather was a man of intelligence and influence in his day. Well versed in scripture knowledge, a citizen inspiring the confidence of his neighbors. He represented his district in the State Senate. Judge Robert Moore, Jr., the father of Mrs. Pomeroy, received this title in being elected to the office of Associate Judge of Montour county. Mrs. Pomeroy's mothers maiden name was P. Ellen Girton. The family came to the north branch from New Jersey.

CHILDREN OF JOHN JAY AND MARY H. POMEROY.

Robert Moore Pomeroy; born April 20, 1870, at Upper Octorara parsonage; deceased Sept. 5, 1870, at Danville, Pa.

Anna Elizabeth Pomeroy; born Aug. 16, 1871, at Upper Octorara parsonage.

Thomas Wilson Pomeroy; born Feb. 4, 1873, at Upper Octorara parsonage.

Edwin Moore Pomeroy; born Nov. 29, 1875, at Rahway, N. J.

Sarah Louisa Pomeroy; born Nov. 12, 1878, at Rahway, N. J.

COPY OF TESTIMONIAL TO JOHN JAY POMEROY, AS CHAPLAIN, FROM THE OFFICERS OF 3D REGIMENT, P. R. V. C.

Headquarters 3d Regiment P. R. V. C., 〉
Near Lewisburg, Va., May 29th, 1864. 〉

The undersigned officers of the 3d Regiment Penn'a Reserves would hereby testify their deep sense of gratitude for and appreciation of the services of Rev. John J. Pomeroy, who for upwards of eighteen months has been connected with the Regiment as its Chaplain.

In offering this slight testimonial, they wish to be understood as not uttering "mere words of course," but are prompted by a desire to convey a heartfelt expression of regard for one who, ever zealous and active, neglected no duty, but on the other hand allowed a christian spirit to prompt him to many acts of charity and benevolence beyond the sphere of his requirements. Upon the field of battle he was always present, assisting the medical officers and tasking his strength to the utmost in efforts to alleviate the sufferings of the wounded.

Among the men of our command we are satisfied there exists a grateful reverence for his inestimable qualities as a christian and a true gentleman. And it is with an echo of the same feeling in our own breasts that we now part with him

at the expiration of our term of service, happy if he will allow us to regard him as our mutual friend.

    •   H. G. Sirkel, Col. 3d Reg't P. R. V. C.,
Commanding 3d Brig., 2d Div., Dept. W. Va.

H. S. Jones, Lieut. and Adjt. 3d Pa. Res.
Acting Asst. Adjt. Gen'l, 3d Brig., 2d Div., Inf'y, D. W. Va.

Rob't Johnson, Captain Co. E.,
Commanding 3d Reg't Pa. Reserves.

Edwin A. Glenn, Lieut. and Act'g Adjt.
3d Reg't P. R. V. C.

John Stanton, Capt. Co. G,   "   "   "   "
Warren Moore,   "   " B,   "   "   "   "
W. W. Satten,   "   " C,   "   "   "   "
John H. Crothers, 1st Lieut. Co. C., "   "   "
J. Jones,   2d   "   "   "
Wm. M'Carty,   2d   "   " H.,   "   "   "
S. J. La Rue,   Captain   "   I.,   "   "   "
Jackson Hutchinson, 2d Lieut. "   "   "   "   "
Albert P. Moulton, Captain   "   F.,   "   "   "
Henry S. Moulton, 1st Lieut. "   "   "   "   "
A. N. Seitsinger,   1st   "   " A.,   "   "   "
Daniel Setley,   2d   "   "   "   "   "   "
Andrew J. Stetson,   Captain " D.,   "   "   "
Albert Broner,   1st Lieut. "   "   "   "   "
Geo. B. Davis,   2d   "   "   "   "   "   "
Thos. H. Bramford, 1st   "   " E.,   "   "   "
Thos. C. Sparkman, 1st   "   " K.,   "   "   "
John M. James,   2d   "   "   "   "   "   "
Samuel Beatty,   1st   "   " I,   "   "   "
William P. Smith, Sergeant Major,   "   "   "

At the close of the war, after the 198th Penn'a Regiment had returned to Camp Cadwalader, at Philadelphia, Pa., a

handsome gold watch was given to John J. Pomeroy, with this inscription:

Presented to the
REV. JOHN J. POMEROY,
Chaplain of the 198th Regt. P. V.,
as a token of esteem, by the
Non-Commissioned Officers and Privates
of the Regiment.
March, 1865.

The following acknowledgment was made by the Chaplain in *The Press:*—

TO THE NON-COMMISSIONED OFFICERS AND PRIVATES OF THE 198TH REGIMENT, PENNSYLVANIA VOLUNTEERS—*Soldiers:* One of your number has just placed in my hand, as a token of your esteem for me, an exquisitely wrought gold watch, with gold chain and maltese cross attached, manufactured to your order by Messrs. Gill & Grisslie, of this city, at a cost of $350.

During my connection with you as Chaplain of the 198th, I am proud to say that in no one instance has any of your number done or said aught to intentionally wound my feelings or cast reproach upon the sacred cause I represent. On the contrary, in my labors among you in the camp, on the march, on the battle field, in the hospitals to which many of you have been carried, prostrated by wounds and disease, I have felt myself more than repaid for all my toil by the many expressions of gratitude that came from your generous hearts. I had no right to expect a material declaration of your regard for me. Because your offering has come to me freely, spontaneously, I shall esteem it the more. I shall constantly have as my companion the evidence of your gratitude, liberality and good taste. This parting gift is peculiarly sacred to me from the fact that many of your comrades who contributed of their means to procure it have sealed their devotion to our common cause with their hearts' blood. It is a testimonial coming to me from the living and the dead. As such, soldiers, I receive

it, and with an honest pride I shall carry it with me through all the days of my life.

With thanks to God that He called me to preach the gospel to the generous and brave defenders of our government, and with many and continuous prayers for your temporal and spiritual welfare, I am yours truly,

J. J. POMEROY,
Chaplain 198th Regiment P. V.
Philadelphia, No. 819 Arch St., June 10, 1865.

Mary Jane, the eldest child of Thomas and Mary Ann Pomeroy, should properly have appeared at the head of the family of which she is the oldest member, but her family record was not at hand in time, and as the printers wanted "copy" we had to proceed with the material available at the time. While this family is not given in the order of their birth, their respective positions can be ascertained in the family record.

Mary Jane, as all the family were, was born and raised at Roxbury. She received a liberal education at the Seminary of the Misses Pinneo, in Chambersburg, Penn'a. In 1860 she was married to her cousin, S. Davidson Herron, of Pittsburg, Penn'a, where she has ever since resided. Mr. Herron has been engaged all his life in the banking business, and has long been cashier of the Fourth National Bank, Pittsburg, Pa.

S. D. Herron and Mary Jane Pomeroy were married at Roxbury, August 16th, 1860, by the Rev. Isaac N. Hays.

Their children were born as follows:

Thomas Pomeroy Herron born June 12th, 1861.
Charles born January 29th, 1863.
Andrew Wilson born June 6th, 1865.
Elizabeth Wilson born March 10th, 1867.
A son, dead born, Nov. 14th, 1869.
Anna Mary born July 25th, 1871.
Cornelia Davidson born January 8th, 1873.

DEATHS.

Anna Mary Herron died January 13th, 1872.

Thomas Pomeroy, the third son of Thomas and Mary A. Pomeroy, passed his whole life in Roxbury, with the exception of a short time when he was absent at school.

His brother, John J., writes of him:

"In regard to brother Thomas, his life was in the quiet, peaceful channel of commercial life. He had social qualities to make him a successful business man. He had a strong desire to reap the benefits of special studies in the departments of commercial life. In order that he might have an opportunity to do so, I took his place in the store in Roxbury after the close of my first year at Princeton Seminary, the summer of 1859. He spent the most of the summer at Duff's Commercial College, Pittsburg. With his past experience in commercial life, he was prepared to derive benefit from the course through which he passed at Duff's College. When he returned to his place again, and took charge of the store in Roxbury, he was well equipped to go on successfully in the business to which he had devoted himself. He was fond of reading, was popular in his manners, had good judgment, dispatched business with correctness, ease and rapidity. His two elder brothers being away from home, his position was one of responsibility. He met the duties that were laid upon him with right spirit and successfully. When death suddenly took him from us, January 5th, 1862, he was we believe prepared for the call."

We are indebted to Rev. John J. Pomeroy for the following sketch of

LIEUTENANT ANDREW A. POMEROY.

He received his education at the school in his native village, Roxbury, and at the Academy at Fayetteville. He was a youth of active mind and keen moral perceptions. He acquired rapidly in all his mental efforts, and from his boyhood days had positive convictions on questions of religion, morals and civil government.

Before the commencement of the war there was one question distinctly settled in his mind, viz: That human slavery as

it existed in the United States, was an iniquitous institution—
an outrageous sin against God and man. He was so pronounced in this view, this heart conviction, that time-serving
politicians spoke scornfully of him as a "young Abolitionist."
There was another question that he regarded as of first importance, that was still unsettled in his mind, when the dark
cloud of war with its arsenal of destruction burst upon our
land, and compelled him with other young men to think of his
personal duty, when there was a call made for men to enlist
in the cause that would sustain our National Government, viz:
The duty that he owed to his God as the Author and Protector
of his life. In this he knew his duty but was conscious of the
fact that he had not voluntarily and heartily given his heart to
the Lord. He told me with his own lips that he had from necessity hesitated to enlist in the cause of his country until he
had in good faith, sincerely and wholly become a soldier of the
Lord Jesus Christ. The choice of the one thing needful, under divine grace, was deliberately, conscientiously and intelli-
gently reached.

There were strong reasons why he should remain at home to
fill the place made vacant by the death of his brother Thomas,
who died January 5th, 1862. He however felt that the call to
serve his country was imperative, and now that he had made
his peace with God and had the discernment to see that with
the sustaining of the government the institution of slavery
must perish, he was carried into the army on the deep and
strong current of personal conviction of right and duty.

August 4th, 1862, in Chambersburg, Andrew enlisted in
military service. August 9th, 1862, in Harrisburg, he was
mustered into the United States service in Company H, 126th
Regiment Penn'a Volunteers, for nine months. The 126th
was immediately sent to the front to share in the perils of the
battle of Antietam, fought Sept. 16th and 17th. About the
middle of October, when the Army of the Potomac was en-
camped at Sharpsburg, Andrew was prostrated by camp fever,
a remitting fever of a typhus character. The regimental hos-

pital was more than full with sick comrades. In the narrow quarters of an A tent brother Stephen and I nursed him day and night for about two weeks, using the meager comforts that could be secured in camp. Sometimes we were buoyed with the hope that he was much better; again, the raging fever, the stiff coated tongue, the languid eye, led us to fear that his days on earth were about numbered.

We felt that the only hope for Andrews recovery was in having him removed to his Roxbury home which could be reached in two days from Sharpsburg by ambulance. We wrote home for covered spring wagon, with bedding to be sent immediately. As soon as the letter reached home the horses were put to the wagon without delay. Samuel Sentman was the driver, and mother with her yearning sympathizing heart for her sick boy, notwithstanding her physical weakness, with her hands almost paralyzed, determined to accompany the wagon in its mission. They came within a short distance of Sharpsburg the first day and early the following morning drove into camp. I took the responsibility of putting our patient in the wagon before the application for sick leave had been returned to regimental headquarters. On the evening of the second day after leaving camp we had him safely quartered in his old home at Roxbury, where he was tenderly and safely nursed through the perils of the disease that had not yet spent its force.

He started for the army again in restored health, February 11th, 1863, riding my horse "Morgan" from Roxbury to Washington, D. C. He joined his regiment near Falmouth, Va., and was with it in the battle of Chancellorsville. In the advance movement he describes the fording of the Rapidan April 30th. He did as many of his comrades, "I pulled off all my clothes but my shirt which I rolled up to my breast and in this condition crossed the Rapidan with my whole equipments." In the fighting of May 3d, in which the 126th was sharply engaged, Andrew was wounded by a minnie ball striking the tip of his thumb on left hand thence passing through his left arm. The wound was painful and disabled him, but was not serious as no bone was broken. Stephen at the same time had his haversack cut by a

fragment of shell and penetrated by a minnie ball.   The hard
tack was broken up by the missiles. They drew no blood however.

The 126th at the expiration of its term of service was mustered out in Harrisburg May 22d, 1863.   On the 23 1 Andrew
with his arm bandaged and in a sling returned to his home in
Roxbury by way of Chambersburg.

In the draft that was made in the summer of 1863, it so
happened that Andrew was among those called out.   He was
sensitive on the point of returning to the army as a drafted
man.   He paid his commutation as a drafted man and immediately went to work securing volunteers, and with the men he
secured from Roxbury and Amberson's Valley entered the
198th Regiment Penn'a Volunteers as 1st Lieutenant of Company I.   His commission is dated Sept. 14th, 1864; was mustered into U. S. service Sept. 16th.   The 198th was at once
sent to the front and took an active part in the service along
the line in front of Petersburg.

Before the opening of the Spring campaign of 1865, Andrew secured leave of absence for fifteen days.   On his return
he came to our old camp at Hatcher's Run, to find that we
had moved.   The next day he pushed forward in drenching
rain and mud, waded through streams up to the waist and
joined his command March 30th.   I remember greeting him
with a very sad heart, for I had been busy through the night
of the 29th, and was still engaged in burying the dead and
looking after the wounded of our regiment.   In the engagement of the 29th the 198th had about 200 wounded and about
20 killed.

On the morning of March 31st our brigade was held in re-
serve while the 2d and 3d divisions of the 5th corps were put
in advance in the forward move that was now being made in
earnest.   Both these divisions were driven back by the rebels.
They were thrown upon us in the utmost confusion.   We tried
to rally them but they broke off to our right and left, both of
which were unprotected.   We were thus left without even a
skirmish line or picket between us and the rebels, who were

following up this advantage with hot haste. It was to me as an eyewitness a most critical moment. Gen'l J. L. Chamberlain, in command of our brigade, ordered Major E. A. Glenn, who was in command of the 198th, to select at once one of his best officers with a given number of men, and to send forward this officer in charge of these men as skirmishers, to meet and clear the woods of the enemy. Andrew was the officer selected for this perilous duty. The last I saw of him alive was at the head of this column of men, as he passed over the hill to our left. They were soon in the ravine, through which ran Gravelly Run. He pushed through the swollen stream with his men, the water taking them to the waist. He was followed up by our advancing brigade. The rebels retreated as our skirmishers advanced. When the edge of the woods beyond the stream was gained, it was found that the enemy had prepared to make a stand behind temporary works on the other side of the upper field that intervened. When this was reported to the commanding officer, Andrew and his skirmishers were ordered to join their respective companies in the brigade, now near to them. Gen'l Chamberlain's command now was, to form the brigade in line, that was considerably broken in passing through the run, the swamp and woods, and to charge across the fields upon the rebels in their fortified position. The captain of Co. I being absent Andrew had command of it. It was when in the act of commanding his men to go forward from this point where he had been the foremost officer in the Army of the Potomac in advancing upon the rebels, that he was struck by a rifle ball under the left eye and died instantly without a struggle. I had knowledge of this sad event a very few minutes after it occurred, as I was following closely after my regiment in its advance. It was the most fearfully trying moment of my army experience when I met several of his men carrying the lifeless body of Andrew to the rear. As the battle was still in progress—the shot and shell from the enemy were flying around us—I was impressed with the importance of acting promptly in getting the body off the disputed ground. I dismounted, and the men at my request placed Andrew's

body, that they were carrying on a board, on my horse "Morgan." One on either side of the horse supported the body on the board; the third man led the horse, and I, in tears, piloted the way through swamp and woods to the ford. "Morgan" seemed conscious of the burden he was bearing. He took his steps with caution as he went through the swampy section of the wood. Although the noise, confusion and destruction of actual battle were about us, my noble horse, full of spirit, chafing under the excitement of the engagement in which he had taken part, without shying in the least, carried the body to Gravelly Run, where I had it put in an ambulance and taken to the field hospital we had established on the 29th.

Through the special request of my friend Gen'l J. L. Chamberlain who spoke of my application to Gens. Griffin and Warren, I received leave of absence for fifteen days for the purpose of taking the remains of my brother home for burial.

What I had done for others it was now necessary for me to do for the remains of my dear brother. I had his body embalmed at our field hospital on the night of 31st. I left it in charge of Serg't Sam'l Sentman, while I hunted up our regimental wagons, in the darkness of midnight to get Andrew's valise. On the morning of April 1st, I had the body taken in wagon to Humphrey's Station and from thence to City Point by cars. Here I had his blood stained clothing removed and his full dress suit taken from his valise, put on, the coffin made, and had it carried on the steam boat "State of Maine" on the evening of the 2d. We started for Washington early on the morning of the 3d with 400 wounded men aboard. I reached home with my precious charge April 5th, and on the following day, followed by a large concourse of friends and acquaintances, we laid away the mortal remains of our beloved son and brother in the family burial ground at Middle Spring. I cannot speak of our bereavement, the cost of this sacrifice to our family. I prefer to leave others than myself speak of his christian character which he took with him and sustained throughout his military life. As Chaplain of the 198th in which he last served, I had great comfort and encouragement in his manly, consistent, christian

deportment. In the daily journal he kept there is frequently a sentence that shows the life of reconsecration to his Savior, and in that of November 27th, 1864, there is an expression of his desire for the spiritual welfare of his regiment. After making note of the preaching service of the day he states, "An interesting prayer meeting was held in the Chaplain's tent to-night. Oh that the work of Christ may prosper here, especially in our regiment." In these social meetings his voice was heard in prayer. He was known in his regiment as an efficient, moral, christian officer. The voluntary tribute that the company of which he was in command most of the time, that of his Captain James P. M'Quade and his commanding General, Joshua L. Chamberlain give him a name and a standing that he honestly wore, and leave us a precious family inheritance, that may, I hope, inspire the present and future members of our family to guard with eternal vigilance the cause for which his pure and noble life was sacrificed.

To Mr. and Mrs. Pomeroy.

It becomes our painful privilege to transmit to you a copy of the Resolutions adopted by our company, expressive of their sorrow at the loss of your son. Without wishing to intrude upon the sacred sanctuary of private grief, we still desire to render to you some token of our affection for departed worth, and sincerely condole with you in this your sudden bereavement. It cannot but be consoling to you when you recollect that he fell while nobly doing his duty and gallantly encouraging his men. He had the respect of the company while living and now that it has pleased God to remove him from our midst we shall ever remember his kindness as an officer and cherish in a grateful memory a feeling of affection for our fellow soldier. We sincerely trust that He who is the "God of Battles" may sanctify this affliction to your good, and leav-

ing you to His love and mercy we ask you to accept the accompanying Resolutions, and remain,

Yours Respectfully,

SERG'T SAMUEL SENTMAN,
CORP'L WALTER R. BITTNER,
ALVAN E. FARR.

Camp 198th Reg't P. V., April 29th, 1865.

At a meeting of the members of Co. I, 198th Reg't P. V., the following Resolution was made and adopted:

Resolved, That a committee of three be appointed to draw up Resolutions expressive of our sorrow at the death of 1st Lieut. Andrew A. Pomeroy.

The following Preamble and Resolutions were accordingly made and adopted:

Whereas, It has pleased Almighty God, in His All-Wise Providence, to remove from our midst 1st Lieut. Andrew A. Pomeroy, therefore be it

Resolved, That we mourn his loss as that of a brave, efficient and Christian officer who fell while nobly doing his duty in front line of battle.

Resolved, That we share in the affliction of his parents, relatives and friends, and tender to them our heartfelt sympathy in this their sudden bereavement.

Resolved, That while they mourn the loss of a beloved son, we also lose in him a kind and gallant officer and one who possessed the love and confidence of the entire company and of the regiment generally.

Resolved, That a copy of these resolutions be forwarded to the parents of the deceased and that they be published in the Chambersburg REPOSITORY.

SERG'T SAMUEL SENTMAN,
CORP'L WALTER R. BITTNER,
ALVAN E. FARR.

PHILADELPHIA, MAY 24TH, 1865.

MR. THOMAS POMEROY,

Dear Sir: Although a stranger to you I feel as if I must claim relationship with you and all of your family on account

of the strong friendship and affection that existed between your son, Lieut. A. A. Pomeroy, and myself. Although our acquaintance was of but few months, yet by his straightforward way of doing business, and his manly and social intercourse with all around him, I had begun to regard him as a brother, and none could mourn the loss of a brother more sincerely than I did his, in fact he was beloved by the whole company and all his associates in the regiment. He was a good soldier and a good patriot, he fought not for vain glory but for the good of his country, and amid all the trials and temptations of a soldier's life he was a faithful soldier of the cross. Amid all the arduous duties devolving upon him as an officer he never forgot his duty to his Maker, and he fully proved to all around him that it is possible and even pleasant to be a Christian at all times and under all circumstances. His Bible was his constant companion, and during his leisure hours was his principal study. His example was worthy the imitation not only of all young men, but also those of riper years. I mourn his loss as a soldier and as a bosom friend, and the only consolation I have left is that he died at his post nobly battling for his country's rights, and also that he died as he had lived a true and faithful soldier of the cross, and that I think should be a great consolation to you as a father and to his afflicted mother. It is a blessed thing to know that although he is lost to you on earth he has gained that priceless treasure that earth cannot give, a crown of glory that endureth for ever.

Now a word about his brother, our worthy Chaplain. He has performed his mission well as Chaplain of our regiment; he has been untiring in his efforts to improve the moral condition of the command, and we want no better evidence of the success of his labors than the fact that our regiment was often spoken of by officers high in authority, as having the best moral character of any regiment in the corps, and I do not hesitate to attribute our good name in that respect to the untiring efforts and the good counsels of our Chaplain. His course has been such as to command the respect of all that knew him. He has of truth been the soldiers' friend, he has shared in common with

us the hardships and dangers of the battle field, always ready to administer to the wants of the sick and wounded, and to give Christian burial to all that fell on the field, and many a soldier will bless him for his many kind offices while in camp or on the field. His duties have been very arduous on account of having a very large regiment, but he has ever been found at his post and has never been heard to complain and he will carry with him the assurance that the officers and men of his regiment will ever remember him with kindness, and always feel grateful for the many kind attentions received from him during their sojourn together.

In conclusion allow me to condole with you and family for the loss of a son so brave and noble, yet while we are called upon to mourn the loss of the noble and the brave, let us not forget to be grateful for the many blessings we have and shall receive from the result of their labors, our bleeding country has been restored to peace, and one of the greatest evils that ever cursed a nation (Slavery), has been removed. We have fully proven to the world that neither foreign foes nor domestic traitors can destroy our glorious institutions. With brave Christian men in our ranks, with liberty and human rights inscribed on our banners and acknowledging God as our great high priest we can bid defiance to all disturbers of our domestic peace.

My best wishes for the health and prosperity of yourself and family. I am very respectfully your obedient servant.

JAMES P. M'QUADE,

Captain Commanding Company "I" 198th Regiment P. V. 1728 Grayson street, Philadelphia.

TESTIMONIAL LETTER FROM GEN'L JOSHUA L. CHAMBERLAIN, LL.D., EX-GOVERNOR OF MAINE—PRESIDENT OF BOWDOIN COLLEGE, BRUNSWICK, ME.

Before entering the army Gen'l Chamberlain had studied for the ministry in the Congregationalist church and was at the commencement of the rebellion a professor in Bowdoin College. His career in the army was distinguished for courage, ability and unabated, intelligent devotion. After his re-

turn to Maine at the close of the war, he was elected Governor of the State for two successive terms. In 1871 he was elected President of Bowdoin College, an institution that takes rank with the first colleges of New England. This position of honor and responsibility he still fills with credit.

HEADQUARTERS 1st DIV. 5th CORPS, } ARMY OF THE POTOMAC.

.JUNE 30TH, 1865.

THOMAS POMEROY, ESQ., ROXBURY, PA.:

My Dear Sir.—As this army is about to break up and I am reminded anew of the brave and good who have served with me through the hardships and hazards of war, I cannot forbear to address you a line expressive of my high regard for your son, late 1st Lieut. 198th Reg't Penn'a Vols., who fell while gallantly fighting at his post in the battle of the White Oak Road, March 31st, 1865. Be assured, sir, his manly and noble conduct was not unnoticed by his General, nor did he fall without the tears due to so brave and true a man. I must also speak of your other son, Chaplain of the same Regiment, whom I esteem as a man worthy of all love and praise, faithful to every trust, wise and not weary in well doing. You may have a pride, though tinged with sadness, in having given men like these to your country's cause, and though one life was laid down yet such lives are never lost. I honor you—I congratulate you as the father of such sons, and I shall always remember with love and mournful satisfaction their heroism and devotion.

I am, my dear sir, with high regard, your friend and servant,

J. L. CHAMBERLAIN,

Brevet Major General, Commanding Division.

———

Stephen Wilson Pomeroy, the second son of Thomas and Mary Ann Pomeroy, was born in Roxbury, Dec. 16th, 1836. In his boyhood he attended the village school and at intervals assisted in his father's store. He united with the church at Middle Spring on profession of faith, April 12th, 1853, the

Rev. John Moody, D. D., being pastor at that time, as he had been for half a century previous. Pursued his academical studies at Academia under Prof. J. H. Shumaker; entered Lafayette College fall of 1858, graduated August, 1861 Taught one year in Tuscarora Academy before entering college. Served nine months during the war in Company H, 126th Regiment Penn'a Volunteers, Captain J. H. Walker. Was elected Orderly Sergeant soon after enlisting. Entered Theological Seminary at Princeton, September, 1863. Served. in Sanitary Commission at Norfolk, Virginia, summer of 1864. Graduated at seminary, April 24th, 1866. Taken under care of Carlisle Presbytery at Duncannon, Perry county, April 11th, 1865; licensed at Middletown, June 7th, 1865. Supplied Seventh Street church, Harrisburg, Sept. 20th, 1866 to April 12th, 1867. Received call from M'Connellsburg, Green Hill and Wells Valley, Fulton county, October 8th, 1868, and accepted. Ordained and installed at M'Connellsburg, Nov. 6th, 1868. Pastoral relation dissolved April 12th, 1871, and dismissed to Huntingdon Presbytery in order to accept calls from Newton Hamilton and Mount Union. Entered upon duties May 1st, 1871. Installed August 14th, 1871. Pastoral relation with Newton Hamilton dissolved April 9th, 1878. Mount Union took half his time, he subsequently received a call from Shirleysburg for the other half, and was installed pastor of that congregation October 17th, 1878.

On November 27th, 1867, he was married to Miss Euphemia Knox Smith, daughter of Silas E. and Elizabeth W. Smith, of Juniata county, Penn'a. Silas E. Smith was a son of Rev. Thomas Smith, who was so long the respected pastor of the Associate Reformed church at M'Coysville, Juniata county. His son Silas occupied the old homestead until his death, and he was a highly respectable and estimable citizen, who was well known by the writer for many years. His wife, and the mother of Mrs. Pomeroy, was a daughter of Mr. Weir, a prominent merchant in Philadelphia, and an elder in one of the churches of the city, so highly esteemed that the General Assembly of the Presbyterian church then in session in Philadel-

phia, adjourned to attend his funeral. Mrs. Smith was an accomplished and estimable lady. Her first husband was Abraham Mason, son of Dr. John Mason.

Mrs. Effie K. Pomeroy received the most of her primary education in Philadelphia, and afterwards attended the Seminary at Academia. She was born in Juniata, in the Smith homestead, December 15th, 1841. Their children are:

Twin daughters born February 12th, 1869, at M'Connellsburg, Fulton county, but lived only part of the day.

Elizabeth Knox Pomeroy born in Germantown, Philadelphia, June 9th, 1871.

Anna Mary Pomeroy born March 13th, 1874, at Newton Hamilton.

Silas Smith Pomeroy born April 4th, 1876, at Newton Hamilton.

Euphemia Weir Pomeroy born May 11th, 1879, at Mount Union, Penn'a.

The following appeared in the FRANKLIN REPOSITORY of November 25th, 1874:

REBEL INVASION—DISPATCH BEARER, S. W. POMEROY.

PITTSBURG, PA., NOVEMBER 21ST, 1874.

Mr. Editor: While on a recent visit to Rev. S. W. Pomeroy, pastor of the Presbyterian church at Newton Hamilton, Pa., our conversation naturally turned to the experiences through which we had passed in the Army of the Potomac and as dwellers on the borders of Dixie, where Federal and Rebel soldiers in the flow and ebb of our war were both on the soil. In this conversation I asked the parson about the carrying of the dispatch of which mention was made in a recent number of the REPOSITORY. Since your paper with commendable zeal is gathering up historical incidents and facts worthy of preservation, it occurred to me that this personal incident and others similar to it are worthy of a place in your local history. While it appears from Mr. Hoke's communication that several young

men performed the good service of bearing dispatches through the mountains to the telegraph line on the Penn'a. Railroad, thus giving to our authorities at Harrisburg and Washington information of rebel movements in Cumberland Valley, these are substantially the facts of S. W. Pomeroy's performing this duty.

After the mustering out of the 126th Regiment Penn'a Volunteers, of which S. W. Pomeroy and A. A. Pomeroy, his brother, were members, these two young men were at home at Roxbury. On June 28th, 500 rebel cavalry made their appearance in this quiet mountain village. They came with a goodly number of horses that had been taken from farmers in Amberson's Valley. It was Sabbath, yet all day long the village smiths were kept at work shoeing horses. The horses were turned into the meadow of Josiah Fickes, a mile east of the village. Before the morning light came, the rebels took their departure in evident haste. It was on June 29th or 30th, that several of the men of Roxbury walked up to Chambersburg, passed through the guards about the town and staid all night at Miller's Hotel. It was during this night that the rebels were moving rapidly from the pike to Fayetteville, through Scotland and nearest way toward Gettysburg. It was regarded as essential that our State and National authorities should be advised of this ominous movement. Judge Kimmel, learning that a son of Judge Pomeroy's was in town, sent for him. When the Judge had taken S. W· Pomeroy into his office, or what was supposed to be his office, it was a dark and barred room, the Judge, in the presence of another gentleman, not known to young Pomeroy, made known the errand upon which he desired him to go. He agreed to undertake the mission, and start without delay. The Judge cut a hole in the buckle strap of the messenger's pantaloons, in which he placed the paper containing the dispatch to Governor Curtin. The messenger, in company with several of his associates, started for Roxbury. After getting a short distance from Chambersburg, they met persons on the road, returning, stating that the rebel guard at the forks of the road leading to Strasburg and Roxbury

would not let them pass. A flank movement through a hollow, the friendly covering of an intervening wheat field that hid from view of the rebel guard, the creeping forms of the men who were slowly and cautiously making their way along the edge of the field, enabled them to get beyond the point guarded by the rebels. When emerging from their friendly covering they were noticed by the rebels, who leaped on the fence with drawn carbines, signaling halt and threatening to shoot. As the messenger and his companions were now out of range, and were rapidly making the intervening distance greater by more than a double quick, the guard did not fire, and very fortunately they did not pursue. Roxbury was reached by the middle of the day, a walk of fourteen miles without a halt for rest. A lunch is taken in Roxbury. Samuel Sentman, sr., provides a horse. The mountain is crossed into Amberson's Valley by way of "the path." The wagon road was barricaded by the farmers of Amberson's Valley felling trees across it to prevent a second invasion. At Concord the messenger got a second horse from his uncle Wm. R. Pomeroy, which he put to its best speed till he reached Beale's Mill, Juniata county, where he secured a third horse from David J. Beale, and from thence to Academia, where he secured a fourth horse from his uncle Jos Pomeroy. With this fresh horse the remaining six miles to the railroad at Perryville is soon made, and the dispatch, at 9 P. M., about twelve hours (12) after it had been committed to the care of the messenger, is forwarded to Governor Curtin from Perryville. The distance from Chambersburg to Perryville by this route is about 54 miles.

Several incidents connected with the messenger's speedy passage through the mountains and Tuscorara Valley on this important mission, make the trip a memorable one. It was reported that the rebels who had made the recent raid into Amberson's Valley had been resisted near Roxbury by a company of men led by Stephen W. Pomeroy, and that in the fight Stephen had been killed, or as some had it, was captured by the indignant rebels and hung. This report had preceded the

messenger the day before he entered the Valley. Schoolmates with whom he had been associated at Tuscarora Academy, who were on picket duty at the gaps and cross roads, heard the report and gave it currency. When the messenger came at full speed on these squads of emergency men he was challenged as one from the regions of the dead, his uncle's face was wreathed with joy as he saw with his own eyes his nephew whom he had announced but a few hours before as dead, living and full of his mission as he checked his panting horse at his front door. At Perryville, when the dispatch had been forwarded, he sought the house of his kinsman, J. M. Pomeroy, who was temporarily residing there, where he was met with the query, "Steve, is this you or your ghost?" A young lady who lived near the highway that led to Perryville, now known as Mrs. S. W. Pomeroy, was especially overjoyed when she saw the manly form of her chief joy enter the front door, not dead, but alive.

Yours Truly,

HISTORICUS.

Alexander Wilson Pomeroy, the fifth son of this family, was like all the others, reared in Roxbury. After receiving his primary education in the schools of that village, he had the advantages of an academical training at several high schools and Business College. He continued to reside at Roxbury, where he was for some time engaged in mercantile pursuits, until the spring of 1879, when he embarked in the Dry Goods business in Shippensburg. His mother removed to that place in the fall of the same year, and Alexander W., who is unmarried, resides with her.

William C. Pomeroy, the youngest member of this family, repeated the history of his elder brothers at Roxbury, by going to school, and making himself generally useful about the store and farm s. He also acquired a good business education. At an early age, through the influence of his uncle Joseph Pomeroy, he became an assistant in the Juniata Valley Bank at Mifflintown, Penn'a. After several years of service at Mifflin, he was transferred to the branch of that institution at Port Royal,

where he is now acting as cashier with entire satisfaction to all who are interested in the institution. He was married on the 20th of March, 1879, to Ellie B. Crawford, daughter of the late Dr. E. D. Crawford, of Mifflintown, Penn'a. Mrs. Ellie Pomeroy was born June 28th, 1857. Her father was a prominent physician, and a gentleman of intelligence, who was very highly esteemed by all his friends. He served a term in the State Senate with distinction, and was conspicuous for his unbending integrity. Her mother is still residing at Mifflintown, Penn'a, where she is highly esteemed.

Elizabeth, a very interesting daughter of this family, died in childhood.

Anna, the date of whose birth and death will appear in the family record, died in her young womanhood, greatly lamented not only by her own immediate family, but by the whole connection, as well as by a large circle of friends who were warmly attached to her. To a very handsome and prepossessing personal appearance was added a sweet disposition, and every womanly grace, which were rendered more beautiful and harmonious by the influence of deep religious convictions. Her final sickness was short and painful. Anna graduated at a Female Seminary in Harrisburg, Penn'a, and her graduating address, which I have recently had the pleasure of reading, displays ability and scholarship of a high order. I have had a partial promise from her physician who attended her in her last illness, and who knew her intimately for many years, to furnish me with a sketch of her which would do justice to her memory, but I have failed to receive it in time to insert in its proper position. If it should yet come to hand, it will appear in one of the closing chapters. What I have here written I regard as a very feeble tribute to the memory of one so lovely in her character.

FAMILY RECORD OF THOMAS POMEROY.

Thomas Pomeroy, born July 11th, 1801.
Mary Ann Wilson, born May 30th, 1811.

. Thomas Pomeroy and Mary Ann Wilson married. March 18th, 1832.

Mary Jane Pomeroy, born December 8th, 1832.

John J. Pomeroy, born September 8th, 1834.

Stephen Wilson Pomeroy, born December 16th, 1836.

Thomas Pomeroy, born January 15th, 1839.

Andrew Alexander Pomeroy, born September 10th, 1841.

Elizabeth Pomeroy, born January 22d, 1844.

Alexander Wilson Pomeroy, born August 4th, 1846.

Anna Elizabeth Pomeroy, born June 17th, 1849.

William Pomeroy, born November 24th, 1851.

Elizabeth Pomeroy, died August 25th, 1848, aged 4 years 7 months 3 days.

Thomas Pomeroy, died January 5th, 1862, aged 22 years 4 months 25 days.

Andrew A. Pomeroy, killed in battle, March 31st, 1865, aged 23 years 6 months 21 days.

Anna E. Pomeroy, died November 1st, 1869, aged 20 years 4 months 14 days.

CHAPTER IV.

Joseph Pomeroy, third son of John and Elizabeth Nevin Pomeroy, was born in Lurgan township, Franklin county, on the 18th day of October, 1804. Like his brothers, with one exception, his education was limited to the common schools of the neighborhood. At an early age he went, as a boy to learn the business, to the store of Stephen Culbertson in Shippensburg, where he remained several years, and acquired a good knowledge of merchandizing, which he pursued mainly throughout life. He began business in Shippensburg before he was of age, but soon sold out, and went to Concord, Franklin county, to take charge of a store for his uncle David Nevin, which he conducted successfully for about three years, when he and his brother William R. purchased the stock, and continued the business in partnership for six years from 1829 to 1835, when William R. retired from the firm. They kept a general country store, and although their business could not be called large, they made and saved a few thousand dollars each during the term of their partnership. From 1835 to 1842, Joseph Pomeroy conducted the business on his own account, and it continued to be successful in its results, and he added each year steadily to his gains. In 1842 he, in connection with William R. and John M. Pomeroy, erected the tannery near Concord, and they conducted the store and tannery very successfully for five years. In 1847 the firm dissolved, Joseph Pomeroy taking the tannery exclusively, where he continued to reside until 1851, when he removed to Academia, where he continued to live until his death

September 21st, 1874. Having purchased several farms and mills near Academia, the care of these, in connection with his store, made his life a very active and busy one. With the assistance of his brother he continued a moderate business at the Concord tannery until the time of his death. He inherited nothing of any account from his friends, which indeed may have been a fortunate thing for him, as inherited wealth is frequently a curse rather than a blessing. He was a man of much more than ordinary energy, with sound discriminating judgment, and unusually cautious in his movements. He was a man of imposing personal appearance, and good address, and these added to his other qualifications, account in part for his financial success.

Concord, where Joseph Pomeroy passed more than a quarter of a century of his eventful life, is situated in the extreme northern corner of Franklin county, among the Blue or Kittatinny Mountains, and is considered an obscure point, being difficult of access, and remote from the great thoroughfares of trade and travel. To get away from it, except to the north, high and steep mountains have to be crossed in all directions. But it was a good point for business, being a kind of centre for a considerable extent of country, and far removed from the competition of large and more important business points. The difficulty of transportation was more than counterbalanced by the increased profits that could be realized on merchandize. As a point for conducting a large tannery, the location was very favorable, the surrounding mountains and wooded valleys affording a sufficient supply of bark for tanning purposes, and for many years there were more than five hundred cords of bark consumed annually in running the tannery. There was a good water power there, and other favorable surroundings for the successful prosecution of the business. The place is a healthy one, fevers and other epidemics scarcely ever appearing. The mountain scenery is as wild and beautiful as any I have seen anywhere, but like the people who live at Niagara Falls, and never hear the roaring of the cataract, many of the dwellers of

this mountain region are partially insensible to the grand and imposing scenes of nature by which they are surrounded. What nonsense to talk about making a voyage to Switzerland to gaze at the mountains, when the traveller can see the wildest mountain scenery to be found on the face of the globe among the blue hills of our own native state. This is the place, and these the scenes, where the subject of this sketch lived for so many years, and these the invigorating influences, and pure mountain air, under which the writer grew from childhood to manhood, and the deceased as long as he lived entertained nothing but pleasant recollections of his old home in the mountains, while the writer looks back to those days of boyhood with pleasurable emotions, and tender regard for the memory of many friends who have passed away.

The subject of this sketch was not unknown to fame as a public man. The same energy which he threw into his business pursuits made him an active member of the Whig and Republican parties. At an early age he made his *debut* as a candidate for Auditor in Franklin county, and was elected. In 1839 he was nominated for the legislature, and although he received the highest vote on the Whig ticket, was not successful. In 1840 he was again a candidate, and was elected, the popular hurrah for "Tippecanoe and Tyler too" sweeping every thing before it and carrying General Harrison into the presidential chair by an overwhelming majority. In 1841 he was nominated for the third time, but the Whig ticket was again defeated in Franklin county and he fell with it. In 1856, having removed meanwhile to Juniata county, he was nominated by the Republican party for Congress in the district composed of Bedford, Fulton, Franklin, Adams and Juniata. The district gave a Democratic majority of about 500 for the state and local tickets, and elected their candidate for Congress. In 1861 he was elected Associate Judge of Juniata county, being the only candidate on the Republican ticket who was successful. This position he held for five years. He always ran well, particularly among his neighbors, and when he was defeated on any ticket it was because the party was in the minority at the polls. He represented

his Congressional district in the Convention of 1872, which nominated Grant and Wilson for President and Vice President.

Joseph Pomeroy was in 1826 married to Eleanor Maclay of Concord, with whom he lived twenty years, she having died in 1846. She was a woman of more than ordinary mental endowments, of deep and active piety, and quite attractive in her manners and person. The writer by the loss of his parents in childhood, became a member of her family when about five years of age, and grew to manhood with her. It affords him the highest pleasure to testify to her intelligence and worth, and to express the regret that one so gifted could not have been allowed by the Supreme Ruler to remain longer with us. By this marriage there were four children, two of whom, Arabella and Robert, both bright and attractive children, died in infancy. In 1847 he was married to Ann Crawford of Concord and three of their children survive. She was an intelligent and pious woman, and died in 1854. In 1856 he was married to Mrs. Jane McGinley of Lurgan township, Franklin county, who died in 1866, much lamented by the members of the family connection. In 1868 he was again married to Miss Mary Stewart of Shippensburg, a lady of excellent qualities, who still survives.

He left an estate of over one hundred thousand dollars.

IN MEMORIAM.

At Academia, Pa., on Saturday, September 21st, 1874, Hon. Joseph Pomeroy, aged seventy years. Mr. Pomeroy was born near Roxbury, Franklin county, Pa., on October 18, 1804. At an early age he was possessed of a spirit of self-reliance and independence, which so conspicuously characterized his whole life. Although a self-made man, yet by his untiring industry and indomitable perseverance, he became successful in business, influential in society, and by the blessing of God, a faithful worker in the church. He was one of the old style of men and merchants—unpretentious, honest, reliable—exact in all his business dealings, whose word was as good as his bond. He had the confidence and esteem of all who knew him. His name and example were a power for good in the

community. His character was most attractive to those who were brought socially in contact with him. In his home he was entertaining and exceedingly hospitable. In his intercourse with his fellow-men he united in himself those qualities of decision, firmness, affection and thoughtfulness of others which endeared him to many hearts. He occupied at his death several positions of responsibility. As a Trustee of Tuscarora Academy, he manifested a deep interest in its usefulness and success, and treated kindly all its students. He was an earnest advocate for a liberal, Christian education. As President of the Juniata Valley Bank, he exhibited prudence and wise management in its affairs—showing, by his great experience and wise judgment, his ability as a skilful financier. As an elder in the Lower Tuscarora church, having been elected in the year 1856, his Christian influence was much felt. Though not having the physical activity to labor effectively in the Master's vineyard, yet by his counsels and in his prayers he made the Saviour's cause a matter of earnest, anxious consideration. In his last illness his thoughts constantly dwelt upon the temporal and spiritual interests of his church, which being without a pastor, made him feel concerned about its welfare. He had great confidence in the disposition of his Christian brethren to do what was right, and he acted upon the promise that all things shall work together for good to God's people. At the last regular meeting of the session the following resolution was unanimously adopted:

Whereas, Our brother, Joseph Pomeroy, is absent from us by reason of sickness and physical suffering, we, the session, desire to express our sympathy for him in this the time of his affliction; therefore,

"*Resolved,* That we freely testify to his worth and activity as a member of the session, and recognize his usefulness as an earnest laborer in the church of which we are overseers. We tender to him the consolations of the Christian religion, and pray that he may sweetly feel in his own experience that God is his helper and the Holy Spirit his comforter."

Thus has Judge Pomeroy passed away—a man devoted to

what was right, conscientious in the performance of duty, of strict integrity, of exemplary character. In him the poor have lost a friend, for no one can say that he was hard upon those who, being unfortunate, struggled in the path of rectitude to success. The community have lost a citizen who was virtuous, high-toned, kindly disposed, correct in his business habits. The church has lost one of its pillars. He had at heart its peace and prosperity. He loved to meditate upon the fact that his church had received so many special tokens of Divine favor. As his days decreased his faith increased and brightened, in prospect of the heavenly land. He sunk at last calmly and easily, his hopes founded on God's Word, in full assurance of the Saviour's love.

> "When faith and love, which parted from thee never,
> Had ripened the just soul to dwell with God,
> Meekly thou didst resign this earthly load
> Of death, called life, which us from life doth sever,
> Thy works and alms, and all thy good endeavor,
> Stayed not behind, nor in the grave were trod;
> But, as faith pointed with her golden rod,
> Followed thee up to joy and bliss forever."

—Presbyterian.

OBITUARY.

Joseph Pomeroy, who died at his residence at Academia, Juniata county, Penn'a, on Monday, the 21st inst., was born near Roxbury, Franklin County, October 18th, 1804, at which place three generations of his ancestors had preceded him, his great grand-father having located in Lurgan township soon after the year 1730, among the first white settlers of Cumberland Valley.

The family are of Huguenot origin, his earliest ancestor, of whom we have any account, having escaped from Paris on the night of the massacre of St. Bartholomew, and found refuge in Ireland, from whence one of his descendants immigrated to America, and settled near Roxbury, where some of his offspring have resided continuously to the present time.

At an early age the subject of this sketch entered the store of the late Stephen Culbertson, in Shippensburg, and after re-

maining several years with him—of whom he always spoke in terms of the highest respect and regard—he went to Concord in this county in 1826, to take charge of a store, sent there by his uncle, the late David Nevin of Shippensburg, which he conducted successfully for three years, when he and his brother William R., who still lives at Concord, entered into the mercantile business together; and subsequently it was conducted, for several years, by himself. He afterwards enlarged his business by the erection of an extensive tannery at Concord, when his brother and nephew became partners with him, and continued the business together for several years. At the dissolution of the firm, Joseph Pomeroy purchased the tannery, and he continued the business, in a moderate way, to the time of his death. In 1851 he removed to Juniata county, having made large purchases of real estate there, which he managed personally, in connection with his store and mills, until his final sickness. He was President of the Juniata Valley Bank and its branches, and was identified with all the religious and benevolent movements of his neighborhood. He was a man of extraordinary energy and force of character, with rare business capacity, which enabled him to accumulate, from a small beginning, a very large estate.

In 1840 he was elected to the Legislature from Franklin county, but failed with his ticket in 1841. He was the Republican candidate for Congress in 1856 in this district, composed of Adams, Franklin, Fulton, Bedford and Juniata. In 1861 he was elected Associate Judge of Juniata county, being the only Republican on his ticket elected, and served the term of five years.

Joseph Pomeroy added to unbending honesty and the strictest integrity, the highest style of Christian character. When yet a boy he made a profession of christianity, and throughout his long and eventful life he never neglected, in the midst of his extensive business engagements, to give full time and attention to the discharge of his duties to the church, and the religious and benevolent operations of the day. For many years he was an active and devoted Ruling Elder of the Pres-

byterian Church, adorning, by his walk and conversation, the Christian religion, and he has no doubt gone to reap the rewards of a life which was spent throughout in the service of his Maker.

—*Franklin Repository.*

John Nevin Pomeroy, the oldest child of Joseph Pomeroy and Eleanor Maclay, was born in Concord. After having spent several years at the school in that village, he went to Tuscarora Academy where he received an excellent business education. His father having removed from Concord to Academia about the time he completed his education, he went into his father's store, and became thoroughly acquainted with the mercantile business. With the exception of five years, in which he filled the office of inspector in the Custom House, at Philadelphia, he has all his life been engaged in merchandizing at Philadelphia, Parkesburg and Academia, where he removed after the death of his father, whose executor he is. He is successfully prosecuting the business of merchandizing, milling and farming at the old homestead, and finds time for actively engaging in the Sunday school and other church work. He is also President of the Juniata Valley Bank.

He was married to Isabella J. Kelly, a sister of Rebecca C. Kelly, the wife of the writer of these sketches. It may not be uninteresting to state that there appears to be a strong inclination among the members of the Pomeroy family to marry sisters. There are at least several examples of this kind in the recent history of the family. The marriage of the second Thomas and his brother, Col. John, to the Misses Graham, in the last century, has already been referred to. Joseph Pomeroy and his brother, William R., married sisters. Then there is the case just stated of John M., and J. Nevin Pomeroy, cousins, married to sisters. The most recent case in point is the marriage of A. Slemmer and William C. Pomeroy, cousins, also, to the Misses Crawford.

Elizabeth Nevin Pomeroy, daughter of Joseph and Eleanor Pomeroy was born at Concord. Graduated at the Mount Joy Female Seminary, was married to Jeremiah Frankhouse, and now (1880) resides on a farm in Beale township, Juniata County.

Eleanor M. Pomeroy, the oldest daughter of Joseph Pomeroy and Ann B. Crawford, was born at Concord, received a liberal education, was married to John T. Nourse, Esq., and now resides on a farm in Spruce Hill township, Juniata county, bequeathed her by her father.

Samuel C. Pomeroy, only son of Joseph and Ann Pomeroy, was born at Academia, and he has lived nearly all his life at Academia, where he is now located on a farm. He was married to Miss Agnes Van Dyke.

Mary Pomeroy, youngest daughter of Joseph and Ann Pomeroy was also born at Academia. After her father's death she married Dr. David Maclay of Greenvillage, Franklin county, where she is living in 1880.

FAMILY RECORD OF JOSEPH POMEROY.

Joseph Pomeroy was born Oct. 18, 1804. Died Sept. 21, 1874.

Was married to Eleanor Maclay, July 11, 1826; to Ann B. Crawford, May 5, 1847; to Jane E. M'Ginley, Jan. 13, 1857; to Mary Stewart, Aug. 27, 1868.

CHILDREN.

John Nevin Pomeroy was born Sept. 26, 1833.

Arabella Erwin Pomeroy was born Nov. 28, 1835. Died April 12, 1839.

Elizabeth Nevin Pomeroy was born Dec. 11, 1837.

Robert Maclay Pomeroy was born Aug. 19, 1842. Died July 27, 1845.

Eleanor M. Pomeroy was born Feb. 15, 1848.

Lydia K. Pomeroy was born Sept. 23, 1849. Died Sept. 5, 1850.

Samuel Crawford Pomeroy was born June 1, 1851.

Mary Pomeroy was born March 30, 1855.

Eleanor M. Pomeroy died July 18, 1846.
Ann B. Pomeroy died Oct. 11, 1855.
Jane E. Pomeroy died Nov. 17, 1866.

Jerry Frankhouse and Elizabeth N. Pomeroy were married January 5, 1857.
Joseph Pomeroy Frankhouse was born April 24, 1859.
Adrienne F. Frankhouse was born Feb. 26, 1862.
Eleanor Maclay Frankhouse was born May 12, 1867.
Elizabeth Nevin and Mary Stewart Frankhouse were born Feb. 16, 1870.
Charles David Frankhouse was born July 21, 1873.
William Reynolds Frankhouse was born March 21, 1875.
Agnes Van Dyke Frankhouse was born July 30th, 1877.

Mary Stewart Frankhouse died December 3, 1872.

———

John Nevin Pomeroy, the youngest with one exception of this family, was born near Roxbury, February 12, 1808, and died at Washington, D. C., on the 24th of April, 1848, aged over 40 years. At an early age he exhibited an ardent desire to procure a classical education, and after the removal of his mother to Shippensburg he commenced the study of the languages under the tuition of different classical teachers in that town. After the necessary preparation he entered Jefferson College at Canonsburg, Penn'a, where he graduated probably about the year 1829. As his means were limited, he was assisted in procuring his education by his relatives, and taught school at intervals to aid him in going through college. After graduating he entered the Theological Seminary of the Presbyterian Church at Princeton, N. J., where he graduated in theology. He was licensed to preach the gospel but was not ordained, and served as a domestic missionary in North Carolina for about a year, and subsequently served, as stated supply, some churches in Perry county, Penn'a, for a year or two. While there he was married to Julia Fulwiler, of Landisburg, Perry county, a most estimable lady, who died about January

1836, leaving one son, William Fulwiler, and an infant daughter Julia. He ceased preaching soon after his marriage, having come into possession of considerable means through his uncle, John Williamson, and also by his wife, and removed to Chillicothe, Ohio, where he purchased the Sciota *Gazette*, a weekly paper which he published some two years.

His business operations in Ohio were not successful, and while there he became imbued with skeptical tendencies on the subject of religion, which, however, he renounced several ye irs before his death, and died in the faith of the gospel. He was a man of solid mind and more than ordinary ability, a strong writer and forcible public speaker. Having been a student from the first and having no opportunity to acquire business habits or experience, he, like many others who pored over books in their early years, found himself without the requisite qualifications to conduct successfully any business enterprise in his riper years.

Returning from Ohio in 1835, he went into merchandizing with his brother, William R., at Mount Union, Huntingdon county, Pa., but his wife dying soon afterwards they did not long continue in business there. He then went to Philadelphia and engaged in teaching classical schools, a vocation for which he was peculiarly well adapted, until his hearing began to grow indistinct. He had charge of the Academy at Milestown, Philadelphia, and subsequently at Sumneytown, Penn'a. About this date he was married to Hannah Slemmer, of Norristown, Penn'a, a worthy partner of his joys and sorrows, who still survives. In the year 1844, having received an appointment as clerk in the War Department, he removed to Washington City, where he continued until his death in 1848.

He delivered the annual address before the Literary Societies of Marshall College, at Mercersburg, Pa., in 1846, which was highly spoken of as a literary effort. In person he was unlike his brothers, being full six feet high, rather raw-boned and the opposite of corpulency, with Roman nose and prominent features. He was a man of pure morals and character, of genial manners and habits, and very fond of his relations.

He had the family mark of deafness, which developed itself in his case, as well as in his brother William, after they were thirty years of age. During the last years of his life he used an ear trumpet, through which he could hear ordinary conversation readily. He was buried at Washington, but his remains were subsequently removed to the cemetery at Norristown, Pa. The children who survived him by his first wife were William F. and Julia, and by the second wife, Margaretta, Joseph and A. Slemmer.

From the address before the students of Marshall College, before referred to, we give the following

BRIEF EXTRACT:

"The natural sciences can, of themselves, effect nothing for the cause of religion. Nature points out no plan of redemption, and no mode of pardon and forgiveness, and throws no light on the darkness of the tomb. No cheering light glitters from the gloomy caverns of the grave, nor can any strong hope of a happy immortality enter the mind. Unaided reason cannot, in the works around us, find out the Almighty. Man can take his flight through the Heavens, and view countless other worlds, all governed by established laws; but he cannot behold Him whose arm is abroad on the universe. He only sees the works of His hands. The false and ridiculous systems of paganism, prove the insufficiency of nature's teachings. Some of the profoundest natural philosophers have denied the very existence of Him who made and governs all; and this proves the inadequacy of nature's instruction. From the very order and harmony of nature, they have been led to dethrone the Almighty, and place nature herself on the throne, and make her their Deity. To him who has right principles and views, every new discovery in the physical world, is an exhibition of the Creator's wisdom and goodness. Admiration and gratitude fill his heart. But the study of physical science alone, will not produce these principles and views. To the benevolent, every species of natural science is regarded as the foundation of some art beneficent to man. To him, the highest glory of

natural science is, in improving the condition and alleviating the miseries of mankind. But the study of physical science itself, is not particularly adapted to inculcate a spirit of benevolence.

The Creator, who is the author of all science and knowledge, has his established laws, and regular operations in the mind and heart, as well as in the material world. These laws, or truths, are as unchangeable as the throne of the Almighty.

The study of the mind shall yet furnish the torch which will illumine the past, and light up and explain much that is now dark and meaningless. It will give a key to unlock much that is now hidden in man's ways. Much of German talent is now employed in these studies, and though errors are consequently published, new truths will be discovered. We need more truths than Locke, Reid, Stewart and Browne have published, in mental science; and we need more light, than such writers as Paley, and our American Wayland, have thrown on ethics. These writers are all, indeed, radically and essentially erroneous and defective.

There is a great disposition among us to place matter above mind. We expatiate on the immensity of creation, and on millions of other worlds, and then turn to man's insignificancy. It is then forgotten, that man's mind is of more importance than mere lumps of matter, and all worlds. It will survive them all. It now measures the weight, dimensions and orbits of worlds, and thus shows its ascendency over them. We speak of the falls of Niagara as grand and sublime, and are apt to forget that the human mind is a far more grand and sublime object. Every law of nature is exercised in the gentle rivulet that murmurs through the grove, that is exercised in the falls of Niagara, and just as much Divine power and goodness are displayed in the former as in the latter. The fact that the falls of Niagara enlarge, very much, a man's ideas of the Divine power, is but an evidence of his mental weakness. Man, with plenty of powder and other physical means, such as mere money could provide, could utterly destroy the phenomenon of the cataract of Niagara, or could, at least, change it into a

succession of cascades. It should never be forgotten, that mind and morals are as far above matter and physical truths, as Heaven is above earth; and our views of mind and morals must become more elevated, and our interest more absorbed, if our literature advance.

Gentlemen, you live in a glorious age, and stand on a noble soil. In this enlightened period, and in this exalted land, you are receiving the best education that our country can afford. Few, comparatively, in our day, enjoy the same advantages; and oh! how Socrates and Plato, Cicero and Demosthenes, would have rejoiced to live in an age like this, and be permitted to know what you may know, and to accomplish what you may accomplish! Your pursuits are lofty, and may afford pure and elevated pleasure. A vast world of thought opens wide before you. The field of science and literature is spread out before your admiring gaze; not dark as once, but well lighted up with torches. In this seat of learning, you are furnished with chart and compass, to steer your way."

———

William F. Pomeroy, the oldest child of John N. and Julia Pomeroy, was, after the death of his mother, placed in charge of his Aunt Mary Pomeroy. He attended the primary school in Roxbury, and when about twelve years of age went to Tuscarora Academy, where he remained some two or three years preparing for college. He then entered Marshall College, where he about completed the full course, but did not regularly graduate, his habits unfortunately being rather intemperate. He then went to the Southwest, taught school in Arkansas, and after leaving a place in that State where he had been teaching was not heard from afterward. His subsequent history is shrouded in mystery. He was a young man of far more than ordinary, and even of brilliant talents.

Julia, the only daughter of John and Julia Pomeroy, was also raised with her brother by her Aunt Mary. She received a good education at the Chambersburg and Tuscarora Seminaries, and was married to Mr. Samuel E. Samuel, of Columbus, Ohio, in 1857 where she still resides.

Margaretta, the oldest child of John N. and Hannah Pomeroy, has resided continuously with her mother in Norristown.

Joseph has been engaged generally in merchandizing, except about five years, in which he acted as editor of the *Saturday Local,* and local editor of the *Franklin Repository* at Chambersburg, Pa. At present he is engaged in the drug business with his brother-in-law S. E. Samuel, at Columbus, Ohio.

A. Slemmer has resided at Norristown ever since his father's death, and has for several years been engaged with his uncle, Charles Slemmer, Esq., in a book store. He was married in 1873 to Margaret E. Crawford, daughter of Dr. E. Darwin Crawford, of Mifflintown, Penn'a.

FAMILY RECORD OF JOHN NEVIN POMEROY.

John N. Pomeroy, born February 12th, 1808.

John N. Pomeroy and Julia Fulwiler, married July 24th, 1832.

William F. Pomeroy, born January 3d 1834.

Julia A. Pomeroy, born January 26th, 1836, and her mother Julia, died February 2d, 1836.

John N. Pomeroy and Hannah Slemmer, married January 9th, 1843.

Hannah Slemmer, born October 9th, 1813.

John N. Pomeroy died April 24th, 1848.

Margaretta S. Pomeroy, born January 9th, 1844.

Joseph Pomeroy, born September 22d, 1845.

Adam Slemmer Pomeroy, born July 9th, 1847.

Adam Slemmer Pomeroy was married February 5th, 1873, to Margaret E. Crawford, daughter of Dr. E. Darwin and Pamelia Crawford, of Mifflintown, Juniata county, Pa.

Edith Pomeroy, daughter of A. Slemmer and Margaret Pomeroy, was born October 31st, 1878.

Samuel E. Samuel and Julia A. Pomeroy, married at Roxbury September 16th, 1857.

Mary Pomeroy Samuel, born August 1st, 1858.

Carrie Elizabeth Samuel, born August 1st, 1858.

Anna Maria Samuel, born December 21st, 1862.

Julia Fulwiler Samuel, born April 20th, 1866.

Ella Jannette Samuel, born December 7th, 1868.
Elizabeth Nevin Samuel, born June 1st, 1871.
Florence Louisa Samuel, born May 2d, 1876.

DEATHS.

Carrie Elizabeth Samuel died February 24th 1863.
Anna Maria Samuel died February 26th, 1868.
Ella Janette Samuel, July 2d, 1870.

William Reynolds Pomeroy, the youngest member of this family, was born in Southampton township, Franklin county, on the 27th day of November, 1811. His father's residence was then on "Herron's Branch," in said township. His schooling embraced only the rudiments of a common English education. His father died when he was a small boy and his mother removed to Shippensburg, where he resided with her and with his brother, Daniel Nevin Pomeroy, with whom he was learning the tanning business at the time of his death in February, 1827. He remained in the tanyard until 1829, during which time he and a fellow apprentice worked out the stock in process of tanning of his brother's, and perhaps tanned some on their own account. In the spring of 1829 he went to Concord and entered into partnership with his brother Joseph in a store, and they continued the business successfully until 1835, when they dissolved, Joseph purchasing his interest in the store. Some remarks in the sketch of Joseph Pomeroy's life in regard to the location, the advantages and disadvantages of Concord as a place of business and residence, will be equally applicable at this point of this narrative. William R. Pomeroy has lived for a much longer period at Concord than any other one of the family. He has not been there continuously since 1829, but he has resided there without interruption since 1842, and altogether up to the present date (1880) about 44 years, or longer than the average life of man.

In 1835 he began the mercantile business with his brother John at Mount Union, Huntingdon county, but the location at that time proving very unhealthy on account of the preva-

lence of fever and ague, with which he was much afflicted, he closed up his business there after an experience of about two years. In 1839 he went into a store with his brother Thomas, at Roxbury. He and his sister Mary kept house there, and Elizabeth N., William F. and Julia Pomeroy were members of their family. In 1842 he returned to Concord, an arrangement having been made between Joseph, William R. and John M. Pomeroy to form a partnership to carry on the store, and also to build a tannery, and prosecute the business of tanning. The partnership continued until 1847, and was successful, the tanning business during that period being moderately profitable. Joseph Pomeroy during the term of this partnership gave most of his time to the the tanning, and with daily consultation with his brother William, who had a better practical knowledge of tanning, they got along very well with the business. In 1845 he was married to Miss Elizabeth Maclay, of Concord, who died in April, 1874, aged 55 years. She was an excellent wife and mother, and extremely domestic in her inclinations and habits. In 1847 he purchased the store and the real estate connected with it in Concord, and continued the business until 1867, when he retired, and has not since been engaged in any active business. His means are sufficient to afford him more than an ample support.

William R. Pomeroy is possessed of all the qualities which mark the family, strict sobriety, firm integrity and devotion to the right, natural talents, and sound common sense, and warm affection for his relatives. He is a man of generous impulses, ever ready to help a friend, and averse to oppressing, in any way, the poor and unfortunate. His word is as good as his oath at any time, and he is universally esteemed in his own neighborhood for his many sterling qualities of head and heart. He has a fondness for reading, and is thoroughly posted in the current events of the day. He was in younger life a very fine looking man, and was doubtless the best looking member of the family. He has the family mark of deafness, which first began to manifest itself when he was about 35 years of age. He has five children surviving, viz: Arabella Maclay, Robert

Maclay, Elizabeth Nevin, John and William. Arabella is married to James Diehl, and they reside in Adams county, Penn'a. Robert when about sixteen years of age went to Parkesburg, Pa., where he remained several years in the store of J. Nevin Pomeroy, when he removed to Iowa, and is now doing business at Shelby. Elizabeth is at home with her father. John, after graduating at Dickinson College, Carlisle Penn'a, went to Iowa, and is now engaged in business with his brother Robert. William, the youngest, is still with his father at Concord, but is about to enter the Normal School at Shippensburg. They all received a good education.

CHAPTER V.

Of the ancestors of Daniel Nevin, the great-grandfather of the writer of these sketches, I am unable to learn anything, and but little of himself, prior to his residence in this county. He was associated in business with William Reynolds, senior, at the time of his death and subsequently married his widow on the 4th of December, 1770. There were born to them children as follows, viz:

Elizabeth, born December 4th, 1771; married to John Pomeroy on the 12th of May, 1794, and died in 1826.

Sarah, born May 22, 1774; married to Daniel Henderson.

John, born November 21, 1776.

Mary, born June 23d, 1779; married to Mr. Maclay, and subsequently when a widow to Mr. Cook.

David, born February 23d, 1782.

Daniel Nevin died December 6th, 1813, aged 69 years and 3 months, and his widow, Margaret, died May 2d, 1822, aged 80 years and 6 months. Daniel Nevin was born August 28th, 1744, and his wife, Margaret Williamson-Reynolds-Nevin, was born October 24th, 1741. Daniel Nevin lived at the tavern stand on the Strasburg road at Herron's branch. The farm on which his son-in-law, John Pomeroy, lived a few years prior to his death, adjoined this farm below, on Herron's branch, and on the western or Strasburg side of that stream.

At this tavern stand Daniel Nevin found his wife, in the person of Mrs. Margaret Reynolds, a widow, who was then keeping the hotel, and they continued to keep it for some time after their marriage. At this time, before the beginning of the great temperance reformation, the business of hotel keeping was quite respectable, and the keepers of hotels on this great thoroughfare to Pittsburg and the West were men of mark and influence, and wielded as much power as any other class of citizens. Before the day of turnpikes the stream of travel went by way of Shippensburg and Strasburg westward. It was by this route that the army of Washington marched when going to quell the whiskey insurrection in 1794, and Washington himself returned by this route from Bedford and took dinner at the hotel of Daniel Nevin. Persons now living have it from members of Daniel Nevin's family, that Washington and his staff stopped there for dinner and that when asked what they would like to have he replied, "an old-fashioned farmer's pot-pie," which was furnished. Some persons who knew Mr. Nevin personally described him to me as an amiable and intelligent gentleman, a good citizen, held in the highest estimation by the community, and a member of the church at Middle Spring, where his remains repose, awaiting the resurrection of the just at the last day.

Elizabeth Nevin, who was married to John Pomeroy, left five sons and one daughter, whose history has been sketched in the Pomeroy family.

Sarah Nevin, who was married to Daniel Henderson, had two daughters and one son, as follows: Samuel D. Henderson, died April 14th, 1857, aged about 60 years; Elizabeth B. M'Pherson, born January 14th, 1801, died August 30th, 1862; Margaret W. Cochran, died August 24th, 1824, aged 19 years, 3 months and 26 days. Samuel D. Henderson left two sons, Daniel and Stephen C. Henderson. Elizabeth B. M'Pherson had seven sons named William Samuel, Daniel Henderson, John Williamson, George Edward, Samuel Davidson, Benjamin Reynolds, and Theodore Horatio Nevin. All these still survive except William, the oldest, who died when young,

soon after his marriage.

Mrs. Sarah Henderson died April 17th, 1833. Her husband, Daniel Henderson, was born August 22d, 1768, and died September 26th, 1852.

John Nevin was a man of liberal education, having graduated at Dickinson College, Carlisle, Pa., in 1797. The original manuscript of his graduating address is still in the possession of a member of the family. It was copied a few years ago into the *Press*, when edited by his grandson, Capt. W. W. Nevin, and I have a copy of it pasted in the book from which these sketches are mainly copied. His subject was "Domestic Slavery," which he denounced in bold and pungent language, and his position must have been ahead of public sentiment, as the "peculiar institution" was then flourishing, and its advocates were strong and powerful. The following extract from it will give a fair idea of the whole speech:

"The silence of contempt is more suitable than dispute with those who vindicate their right to enslave the unfortunate negroes, by arguing that they are an inferior link of the chain of nature, and therefore doomed to slavery. And yet it is impossible for a considerate and unprejudiced mind to think of this without horror. That a man, a rational and immortal being, should be treated on the same footing with a beast, or piece of wood—bought, sold and entirely subjected to the will of another man, whose equal he is by nature, and whose superior he may be in virtue and understanding, and all this for no crime, but merely because he was born in a certain country, or of certain parents, or because he differs from him in the shape of his nose, the color of his skin, or the size of his lips. If this be equitable, or excusable, or even pardonable, it is in vain to talk any longer of the eternal distinction of right and wrong, truth and falsehood, good and evil."

John Nevin never studied a profession, but settled down quietly on a farm in Letterkenny township, Franklin county. His superior education, and general intelligence and ability, gave him prominence among men, and he was an influential citizen of Cumberland Valley. He was two or three times

the candidate of the Federal party for the Legislature in Franklin county, but as they were always in the minority he was defeated In the later years of his life he removed to a farm near Shippensburg, on which he died about the year 1829, greatly beloved and respected by the whole community. His children were John W. Nevin, D. D. L. L. D., late President of Franklin and Marshall College; Professor William M. Nevin, also of Lancaster; Rev. Daniel Nevin, Theodore H. and Robert Nevin, all of Pittsburg, Pa., and three daughters, married respectively to Dr. Findley, Rev. A. Brown, D. D., and Mr. Irwin.

Mary Nevin was first married to Mr. Maclay, a brother of Robert Maclay, late of Concord, Franklin county. She had two children at least by her first marriage, one of whom was John Maclay, lately, or yet of Alabama, and Margaret, married to John Brookens of Ohio. By her second marriage she had two children, the late Isaac Cook of Western Pennsylvania, who was a Presbyterian minister of more than ordinary eloquence and ability, and his sister, Mrs. Sarah Howe, a widow, of Chicago, Illinois.

David Nevin was the youngest member of this family, and survived the others many years. In early life he removed from Herron's branch, where he was born, to Shippensburg, and began business as a merchant. He subsequently, in connection with his mercantile business, became a large dealer in flour, grain and country produce generally. He also dealt largely in real estate and at the time of his death was possessed of several of the best farms in Cumberland Valley. He was a member of the convention to amend the Constitution of Pennsylvania in 1837, and he was also a prominent and influential citizen. He died May 27th, 1848, aged sixtysix years and three months. His children, who survived him, were Joseph P., (died in 1859), Mrs. Caroline Rankin, Rev. Edwin H. Nevin, D. D., Rev. Alfred Nevin, D. D. L. L. D., Mrs. Jane M. Reynolds, Mrs. Mary P. Tustin, Samuel W. Nevin, Dr. W. W. Nevin, and Major D. R. B. Nevin.

THE WILLIAMSONS.

It will be observed in the preceding sketch of Daniel Nevin, that his wife, who was the common mother of all the Nevins and Pomeroys of our branch of these families now living, was Mrs. Reynolds, a widow, whose maiden name was Margaret Williamson. Her father, John Williamson, was originally a clothing merchant of Dublin, Ireland, who emigrated to this country and settled in West Nottingham township, Chester county, Penn'a., in 1730, where he was married to a lady who was also a native of Ireland, named Mary Davison. He subsequently removed to near Shippensburg, where he died in 1757. His wife died in 1804 at the advanced age of 90 years. His daughter Margaret was married to William Reynolds when quite young by whom she had three children, one daughter was married to Francis Graham, of Roxbury, and another to William Herron. William, the son, was married to a sister of Robert Maclay, of Concord. Their children who grew to mature years were William, John, Charles Maclay, Hugh Williamson, Margaret, married to A. S. McKinney, Eleanor, married to Mr. Plummer, Elizabeth, Nancy and Mary Catharine.

John Williamson, our foreign ancestor, had ten children, but I have no account of any but four of them. His son John lived an old bachelor, and died about 1831 at an advanced age. He was long engaged in mercantile pursuits in Charleston, S. C., and left at his death a very large estate to his numerous relatives. Margaret, a daughter, was Mrs. Reynolds and subsequently Mrs. Nevin. Another brother lived in England, and one of his grandsons is now an Episcopal preacher there, with whom some of the family have recently had some correspondence. A sister of Sir William Wallace, the Scottish chieftain, was married to Mr. Williamson, an ancestor of John Williamson.

Hugh Williamson, LL. D., another son of John Williamson, and brother of Mrs. Margaret Nevin, was one of the most prominent men of the country after the Revolutionary War,

in which he served as surgeon. For a sketch of Dr. Hugh Williamson collected from a fuller history of this eminent man, I am indebted to the Hon. J. Smith Futhey, of West Chester, by whom it was prepared and published as one of a series of papers sketching prominent citizens of Chester county:

HON. HUGH WILLIAMSON, M. D., LL. D.

Hugh Williamson was born of Scotch-Irish parents, in the township of West Nottingham, Chester county, on the 5th of December, 1735. These Scotch-Irish immigrants have been .remarkable in our country for their enterprise, and for the intellectual development of their descendants. His father, John Williamson, (who had been a clothier in Dublin,) came to Chester county about the year 1730. His mother, Mary Davison, was a native of Derry, and came hither with her father, George Davison, when a child of about three years of age. She died about 1804, in her 90th year. The parents of Hugh Williamson were married in 1731. They had ten children—six sons and four daughters. Hugh was their eldest son. Being slender and delicate, his father resolved to give him a liberal education. After the common preparatory instruction, he was sent at an early age to learn the languages, at the academy at New London cross roads, under Rev. Francis Allison,—the Busby of the Western Hemisphere. Among the pupils of that seminary may be mentioned Charles Thompson, Dr. John Ewing, Thomas McKean and Benjamin Rush. After Dr. Allison's transfer to Philadelphia, Hugh Williamson went to the Academy at Newark, Delaware, where he prepared for college. He entered the Philadelphia college in 1753, remained there for about four years and graduated A. B. May 17, 1757. He was fond of mathematics and became a proficient in Euclid. His father, who had, shortly before this, removed to Shippensburg, Cumberland county, Pennsylvania, died the year Hugh graduated, as above; whereupon he became sole executor, and resided with his mother for about two years, settling his father's estate. He became early im-

pressed with a sense of religion, and while with his mother devoted much time to the study of divinity, under the auspices of Rev. Dr. Samuel Finley, with a view to the clerical profession. In 1759 Hugh went to Connecticut, where he still pursued his theological studies, and was licensed to preach the gospel. He preached but a short time—not exceeding two years—when he found that his health and strength of lungs would not permit the duties of the office, and he was never ordained. Moreover, the memorable controversy in the Presbyterian church between the adherents of Whitefield and the old orthodox party, proved a source of disgust to him, which induced him to withdraw from theological pursuits, to which he had become sincerely attached. He accordingly left the pulpit and entered upon the study of medicine.

In 1760 he received the degree of **A. M.** in Philadelphia college; and soon after was appointed professor of mathematics in that institution; but continued his medical studies.

October 8, 1763, he gave notice of his intended resignation of the professorship; and in 1764 he went to prosecute his medical studies at the University of Edinburgh. He afterwards spent a year in London at his studies, and from thence crossed over to Holland, and completed his medical education at Utricht. Having passed the usual examinations and submitted a Latin thesis, he obtained the degree of doctor of medicine. Having spent some time in travelling on the continent of Europe, he bent his course toward his native country.

Upon his return Dr. Williamson practised medicine in Philadelphia for a few years. In 1768 he was chosen a member of the American Philosophical society. His health failing, he resolved to try mercantile pursuits. But meanwhile for a time, devoted himself to literary and philosophical investigations. In January, 1769, he was appointed by the Philosophical society on a committee with the Rev. Dr. Ewing, David Rittenhouse and Charles Thompson, to observe the *transit of Venus*, which occurred on the 3d of June in that year; and soon after to observe the *transit of Mercury*, which took place November

9, 1769. In that year, also, he philosophised on the comet.
In 1770 he published observations on Climate in the "American Philosophical Transactions." In 1772 he visited the West
Indies, to collect contributions in aid of the Newark Academy. In 1773 Governor John Penn certified to the "good
credit and reputation" of Rev. John Ewing and Hugh Williamson, who were authorized to proceed to Europe to solicit
further aid for said academy. They persevered under difficulties until the autumn of 1775, when hostilities with the colo-
nies commenced. Dr. Ewing returned home; but Dr. Williamson resolved to remain, and make further efforts for the
Academy. Dr. Williamson was the first to report the destruction of tea at Boston. On that occasion he ventured to declare
his opinion, that coercive measures by parliament would result
in civil war. Lord North himself declared, that Dr. Williamson was the first person who, in his hearing, intimated the
probability of such an event. Dr. Williamson, while in London, was the man (probably with the aid, or at the suggestion
of Sir John Temple,) who procured the letters of Huchinson,
Oliver and others, and caused them to be delivered to Dr.
Franklin, who sent them to Boston, for which Wedderburne,
before the privy council, called Franklin a "thief"—or in other
words—*Homo trium literarum.* [F. U. R.]

After causing the Huchinson correspondence to reach Dr.
Franklin, it was deemed expedient by Dr. Williamson to take
an early conveyance next day for Holland. It was supposed
by John Adams that Mr. David Hartly, a member of parliament, and a good friend of the Americans, was the person
through whom the letters reached Dr. Franklin. On the Declaration of Independence, Dr. Williamson returned to the
United States, and engaged for a time with a brother in trade
with the West Indies. His residence then was at Edenton,
North Carolina. In 1779–80, when the British took posses-
ion of Charleston, South Carolina, a large draft of military
from North Carolina was ordered for the relief of South Carolina; on which occasion the commander, Gov. Caswell, placed
Dr. Williamson at the head of the medical department. After

the battle of Camden, August 18, 1780, which the doctor witnessed, he requested Gen. Caswell to give him a flag, that he might go and attend to the wounded North Carolina prisoners. The General advised him to send some of the regimental surgeons, inasmuch as his duty did not require him to go. Dr. Williamson replied that such of the regimental surgeons as he had seen refused to go—afraid of the consequences. " But," said he, "If I have lived until a flag will not protect me, I have outlived my country: and, in that case, have lived a day too long." He went and remained two months in the enemy's camp, rendering good service to the sick of both armies, where his skill was highly esteemed. At the close of the war, Dr. Williamson served as a representative of Edenton, in the house of commons of North Carolina.

He was next sent to Congress from " the old North State," where he continued for three years. Writing to President Dickinson, of Pennsylvania, from New York, while in Congress, January 14, 1785, about John Franklin and the other Connecticut intruders, at Wyoming, Dr. Williamson says in the conclusion of a letter:—" I have taken the liberty of giving you a full information, as I cannot cease to feel myself interested in the peace and reputation of a state which gave me birth." In the year 1786, he was one of the few delegates sent to Annapolis, to revise and amend the Articles of Confederation of the union ; and in 1787, he was a delegate from North Carolina to the convention which framed the Constitution of the United States. Dr. Williamson was a zealous advocate of the new Constitution and was a member of the State Convention which adopted it. He served in the first and second congress, and then declined a re-election. In January, 1783, he married Miss Maria Apthorpe, of New York, where he came to reside, and had two sons, who both died young. He continued industriously to write on various philosophical subjects; was an advocate of the great New York canal system ; an active promoter of philanthropic, literary, and scientific institutions ; and in 1812, gave to the world his History of North Carolina. After a long life devoted to the

best interests of humanity, Dr. Hugh Williamson died suddenly, at New York, on the 22d of May, 1819, in the 85th year of his age. Of him it may safely be predicated, that he was an ornament to his country, and one of the most eminent and useful men which the ancient county of Chester has yet produced. For an interesting account of Dr. Williamson see Dr. Hosack's Memoir in the transactions of the New York Historical society.

To the Editor of the Franklin Repository:

A HISTORIC FAMILY.

Previous to the year 1730, no white settler had yet erected his cabin west of the Susquehanna. The Indian tribes, the aboriginal owners of the soil, still remained its sole possessors; and their villages and wigwams were the only evidences of human life which were to be found in the rich and beautiful Cumberland Valley. Yet, from the eastern bank of the river the covetous eye of the pioneer, cast long glances over the fair region which lay beyond, impatiently awaiting the time when he might safely cross over and occupy the land. It was a perilous undertaking, full of danger, yet the daring spirit of the sturdy Scotch-Irish race was willing to accept the risk.

In that year Benjamin Chambers built his primitive log dwelling at the confluence of the Conococheague and the Falling Spring. Simultaneously, the three McDowell brothers settled at the present village of Bridgeport, at which point John erected a mill, which, at a later period, he surrounded with a stockade, converting it into a fort, for protection against the incursions of the Indians, who made frequent murderous forays into this section of the valley, after the disastrous defeat of Braddock in July, 1755. In the same year, 1730, Thomas Pomeroy, the first American ancestor of the Pomeroy family, who have for a century and a-half been

honorably identified with the history of Lurgan township, located in the north-eastern section of the present county of Franklin, near the base of the Kittatinny Mountains. At this period the whole of the Cumberland Valley, called by its dusky owners the "Kittochtinny," and by the settlers east of the Susquehanna, the "North Valley," was then included within the territorial bounds of Lancaster county, which, indeed, embraced all of the province lying beyond the western bank of that river. A few years later, in 1735, the land in this section of Franklin county, was included in Hopewell Township, Lancaster County. In 1741, Hopewell Township, which included all of Franklin County east of the Kittatinny Mountain, as well as a large part of Cumberland county, was further divided into two vast townships, the eastern retaining the original name, Hopewell, and the western, that of Antrim. The date at which Lurgan township was formed cannot be definitely ascertained, but it may be given as 1750, the year in which Cumberland County was erected.

The name of Pomeroy is French, and signifies *royal apple*. The first member of the family of whom any record is preserved, was a Huguenot, who lived in Paris until the ruthless slaughter of French Protestants on Saint Bartholomew's day, in 1572. He was a fine scholar, and was engaged in teaching a classical school at this dark period of religious persecution. On the night of that dreadful day, in company with some of his co-religionists, he escaped to Ireland. His descendants lived in Ireland a hundred years after his death; but of their history we have no particulars. They resided in the province of Ulster. Thomas Pomeroy, the first of the family who came to America, was born in Ireland, but removed to Liverpool, and engaged in mercantile pursuits in that city, before he determined to seek his fortune in the boundless wilds of Penn's distant province. Arriving in America, he pushed boldly into the western wilderness, and finally selected a rich tract of land, about two miles east of Roxbury, through which flowed a small mountain stream, now known as "Rebuck's Run." Near the bank of the stream, about a fourth of a mile from the "State

Road," a highway running from Roxbury to Newburg, he
built his cabin of logs, with its customary huge stone chimney on the outside, and also cleared a small adjacent patch
of land to serve as a garden. Here he lived in quiet isolation
until 1770, the year of his death. In consequence of this
event, his son Thomas, who was born in Lurgan township, in
1733, and had reached the period of mature manhood, now
became the head of the family. All the other sons, three in
number, and three daughters, went further west and settled in
Westmoreland and Mercer counties, and in the Indian wars
which soon followed, the sons became conspicuous for their
military services.

On the ancestral homestead Thomas resided, peacefully cultivating his small clearing and supplying his family plentifully
with the result of his hunting excursions, as the locality
abounded in game of all varieties. His quiet life was ulti-
mately broken by a most unexpected and tragic interruption.
The Indian tribes had been friendly since their severe punish-
ment inflicted by Col. John Armstrong, at Kittanning, in September, 1756. Early in 1763, the celebrated Ottawa Chief,
Pontiac, planned the famous conspiracy which bears his name,
by means of which he hoped to drive the pale-faced intruders
from the hunting grounds of his ancestors. Soon the dreaded
invasion came, and the whole wide region east of the mountain range was devastated by the infuriated savages. The
inhabitants were cruelly murdered and their dwellings destroyed
by fire. Divided into small parties, there was no nook or corner of the valley that they did not visit; and, in a few days, it
was literally depopulated; as those who escaped the tomahawk
and scalping knife sought refuge in Shippensburg, Carlisle
and other places of safety east of the Susquehanna. In the
general destruction, the family of Thomas Pomeroy did not
escape. Near his house was a "lick" to which the deer were
accustomed to resort, and whither Thomas was in the habit of
going to shoot them. In the early morning of July 21st, 1763,
Thomas was at his hiding place waiting the approach of his
unsuspecting game. After a short absence he returned home.

But the Indians had also been there, and left terrible evidences of their sanguinary visit. The lifeless bodies of his wife and two children met his horrified gaze, having been both toma-hawked and scalped by the lurking fiends, who were doubtless hidden in the vicinity, awaiting the expected absence of their protector, whom the savages feared to attack, knowing that some of them would surely fall before his deadly rifle. A Mrs. Johnston, who was at the house at the time, but whether an inmate or merely a visitor, is not known, met a similar fate, but life was not yet extinct upon the return of Thomas. *The Pennsylvania Gazette,* in a brief account of the tragedy, says that this lady, "showing some signs of life, was brought to Shippensburg in a most miserable condition some hours after-ward, being scalped, one of her arms broken, and her skull fractured with a tomahawk." These victims of savage ferocity were buried on the eastern side of the "State Road," and over their graves the barn of the late John A. Rebuck was subse-quently built. A few years ago a small cleared space at the margin of a woods a pile of stones indicated the location of Thomas Pomeroy's residence.

The second wife of this gentleman was Mary Graham, daughter of Francis Graham, Sr., who lived and died on the farm adjoining Roxbury on the east, and now owned by his great-great-grandson, Alexander W. Pomeroy, of Shippens-burg.

Francis Graham, Jr., who was a soldier in the Revolution, inherited this property from his father; but, in his latter days, lived in the small log house, near the homestead, now owned by James Patterson.

A brother of the second Thomas Pomeroy, named John, was also married to a daughter of Francis Graham, Sr., before his removal to Westmoreland county. John Pomeroy became a prominent citizen of the western part of the State, and dis-tinguished himself as Colonel of a regiment of troops in the Indian wars. His other brothers were named George and Samrel; and, as already intimated, became prominent citizens in their new homes.

The entire first family of the second Thomas was, as we have seen, destroyed by Indians. A large second family, resulting from his marriage with Miss Graham, consisted of eight sons and three daughters. The sons were respectively named Thomas, Joseph, John, George, Francis, Charles, James and Isaac. The names of the daughters were, Elizabeth, afterwards Mrs. White; Margaret, who married Mr. Adams, and Mary, who subsequently became Mrs. Caldwell. All these children moved to the western part of the State, except John, Charles and Mrs. White, who remained in Franklin county. John Pomeroy was married to Elizabeth Nevin, of Southampton township, and left five sons and one daughter, all of whom were born in Lurgan township. The names of the sons were Daniel Nevin, father of John M. Pomeroy, Editor of the *Franklin Repository*; Thomas, Joseph, John and William. Mary was the name of the daughter. Of these children the last named son alone survives, and resides in Concord, Franklin county, Pa.

Thomas Pomeroy, the second, died in 1803, leaving several large farms situated near Roxbury, to his children. This gentleman, it will be remembered, was the grandfather of the late Judge Thomas Pomeroy, of Roxbury, who was so extensively and favorably known in this part of Pennsylvania.

It will be observed that during the long period in which the Pomeroy family resided in Lurgan township, at least one member has borne the name of Thomas. Thomas, son of Judge Pomeroy, died in Roxbury in 1862. A young son of Rev. John J. Pomeroy, of Rahway, New Jersey, is the only member of the family by whom it is perpetuated.

During the long lapse of time intervening since the settlement of the first Pomeroy in Lurgan township, 1730, the successive members of the family have been large land holders, and have borne a prominent part in the development of its resources. They have all been distinguished for sterling integrity, rigid morality, and fine business qualifications, which always gave them the first position among the most conspicuous and useful citizens of their section

For many years the late Judge Thomas Pomeroy, then the head of the family, was engaged in tanning and merchandizing, in addition to his superintendence of his several farms. Having relinquished the trade of tanning, he was followed in the mercantile business successively by his sons, Thomas, Andrew, and Alexander W. Pomeroy.

It cannot be otherwise than a subject of regret that, after so long a residence, there are now no members of the family living in their old home; Mrs. Mary Ann Pomeroy and her son, Alexander, having removed to Shippensburg in the spring of 1879. Their large landed estates, however, still remain in the possession of the heirs of the late Judge Pomeroy. Huguenot and Scotch-Irish Presbyterians from the beginning, few or no members of the family have ever felt disposed to renounce the doctrines of the church, as embodied in the Westminster Confession, the faith of their fathers.   L.

Dr. Lane kindly contributed the above to the history at my request.

To the Editor of the Franklin Repository.

A MEMORIAL.

A short time since the writer visited the hallowed locality of Middlespring. He rambled over the old graveyard near the Spring, beneath whose sod the "rude forefathers of the hamlet sleep," and paused over the ashes of slumbering Revolutionary patriots, who fought to insure the independence that we now enjoy. Here the mortal remains of the patriotic Dr. Cooper, who accompanied many of his parishioners, now lying in close proximity, followed the army of Washington in its disastrous retreat through New Jersey, during the darkest period of the uncertain conflict. For many years after the close of the War, he was an equally faithful soldier of the Cross. In this old burial place rest the remains of many distinguished men and women who took an active part in the prominent and momentous events with which the Revolutionary period

was crowded, and whose names have become historical. The graves of those are for the most part unmarked, and cannot now be determined. In this respect it contrasts strikingly with the modern cemetery on the hill, in the rear of the Church, in which numerous marble stones and imposing shafts commemorate the memories and virtues of the later members of the Congregation. Near the western gate, in a square, inclosed by an iron fence, are a row of graves in which many members of the Pomeroy family rest. Among the marble slabs which indicate the names of their occupants is one bearing the following inscription:

Anna E. Pomeroy, the youngest daughter of Thomas and Mary Ann Pomeroy, was born in Roxbury, on June 17th, 1849. Anna Pomeroy possessed in an eminent degree, those estimable qualities of head and heart which win and retain the love and admiration of the world. She was gentle, simple and natural, and was singularly favored by nature with rare physical and mental endowments. She exceptionally combined the winning artlessness of innocent girlhood, with the graceful dignity of the matured woman. There was an irresistable fascination in her presence, which all who came within range of its mystic influence felt and spontaneously acknowledged. To say that she was emphatically the beloved idol of a large acquaintance, is simply, without exaggeration, stating a recognized truth.

She was born in Roxbury, near the foot of the North mountain, in the vicinity of which her ancestors had lived for more than a century. After acquiring the rudiments of an education in the village school, she entered the female seminary of Mrs. Williams, located at Newburg, in Cumberland county. She remained here, making satisfactory advances in her studies, until the school was removed to Harrisburg. A warm reciprocal attachment having sprung up between her and her teacher, Anna followed the school to that city. She remained there until her graduation in the month of June, 1866. Her valedictory essay was styled "A Model Character," and is itself a model of its class, rising high above the usual standard

of such exercises. It is written in simple and classic English, and exhibits a maturity of thought and elegance of diction which are rarely combined in one so young in years, and whose period of study was somewhat limited. It exhibits the finished elegance of the practiced writer, rather ~~that~~ the expected immaturity of the unpracticed school-girl.

In her early girlhood, while in the Newburg Seminary, she gave her pure and youthful heart to God, and attached herself to the Congregation of Middlespring, under the pastoral charge of the Rev. I. N. Hays.

A loving, refined and sensitive girl seems naturally attracted towards her Creator, and her character appears incomplete and inconsistent until she has given her pure heart to her Redeemer. Reading, in the towering peaks of the neighboring mountain—in the rippling waves of the Conodoguinet, on whose banks she was accustomed to stroll in the twilight of departing day—in the majestic forests, the most familiar objects upon which her eyes rested—the evidence of an Almighty hand, she was soon, almost unconsciously, taught to look from these beautiful creations up to the beneficent Creator at whose command they sprang into existence, and gave her heart to him. When the proper time arrived for her to make a public acknowledgment of her duty, by uniting with the church, she discharged this obligation as calmly and cheerfully as she was accustomed to discharge the ordinary duties of her every day life.

Death came very suddenly, and his invasion of the citadel of her peaceful life was very rude and painful. But he came shorn of his terrors, because she firmly trusted in One greater than he, who would aid and rescue her in the dreadful trial. After fearful suffering during three days, she passed gently into the repose of Heaven, bearing bright witness to the last how a confidence in the blood of Christ can divert Death and the grave of their terrors.

Although her life was so short, yet she was an agent through whom God accomplished much good; for her bright example of a holy and unselfish life lingers around the home of her

childhood, like the delicate fragrance of the wild flowers which exhaled their volatile odors in her accustomed haunts in the laurelled bowers on the mountain streams, to which she was wont to resort in her communings with God and Nature.

* * *

———

The following extracts from manuscripts kindly sent me by members of the New England branch of the family, are worthy of preservation in this volume:

Sir Ralph De Pomeroy was a favorite knight, or what moderners would call aid-de-camp, of William the Conquerer, to whom after the conquest of England, he gave fifty-seven townships (farms) in Devonshire and several in Somersetshire, in one of the Devonshire manors. Sir Ralph built a castle, the ruins of which were standing in 1820 in tolerable preservation, and had been visited by numerous antiquarians, which with the domain attached is still (1830) in possession of one of the family. Arthur Pomeroy, a descendant, went to Ireland in the reign of Elizabeth as Chaplain to the Earl of Essex, and then laid the foundation of an estate now held by his descendants, one of whom, Arthur Pomeroy, was ennobled in 1783, by the name of Baron Harburton, of Castle Carberry, and was subsequently created a Viscount, but dying without any issue, he was succeeded by his brother Major General John Pomeroy, who served in the British army during the American Revolutionary war, and was succeeded by his son or nephew Henry, the present Lord of Harburton.

The branch from which the New England family proceeds emigrated from Devonshire about the year 1633, and settled at Dorchester, near Boston. There were two brothers, Eltweed and Eldred, and by the records of Dorchester, Eltweed Pomeroy was a man of some substance, for he owned two cows, no settler had more than three, which was considered at that time a good estate. They are represented as possessing liberal and independent minds and were disgusted with the tyranny of the Stuarts and Archbishop Laud,

hence their removal to America. They subsequently removed with their minister, Rev. Mr. Warham, to Windsor, Connecticut, where the records of the town contain grants of land to Eltweed *Pomry.* The orthography of the name has varied, our ancestors not attending to or caring much about spelling, and often left out letters, Pomry, Pomery, Pomroy, Pumroy, hence the pronunciation attained in many parts of Massachusetts and Connecticut of Pumery. A portion of the name drop the O in spelling, but it is doing murder to one of the handsomest names in the English language. Pomeroy is the true mode of spelling, and should be pronounced as O is in home, and is so pronounced by the family in England and Ireland to this day, being the French for King Apple—Pome, apple—Roy, king. Tradition says there was found on the estate in Normandy, from which Sir Ralph emigrated, a peculiar apple of which some king was very fond, from which circumstance the estate was called King Apple. In those days men took their surnames from the estate on which they were raised, hence Ralph of King Apple, or Ralph De Pomeroy. The general characteristic traits of this family are, a strong attachment to the principles of religious and civil liberty, and the social virtues, great moral and physical courage, and seldom can one be found that is not given to hospitality.

Their arms are a lion in the field rampant, a lion segant (sitting) holding up an apple by the stem in his dexter right paw. Motto—*Virtutis fortuna comes.*

These extracts embrace about all that will be interesting in this connection. The family records sent me by the eastern branch of the family, were useful in supporting the genealogy of our immediate branch of the family as herein given, but it is not necessary to reproduce them here. They also sent me an impression of the coat of arms, which is very accurately described above. I intended to get a cut of it made and print it with these sketches, but neglected it until too late to get it in time. Any member of the family who may want one for his own use, has only to go to a leading stationer in any city, and for the sum of five dollars it will be furnished. If the

above description should not be sufficiently clear and explicit for the engraver, I can furnish an impression received from Robert Pomeroy, Esq., of Pittstield, Mass., who uses it on his letters, &c. He has also the old anvil used by Eltweed Pomeroy, who was a gunsmith.

The commission of John M. Pomeroy, Paymaster United States Army, is dated August 14th, 1861. It is valuable because it has the genuine signature of Abraham Lincoln, the martyr President, and also of Edwin M. Stanton, the great War Secretary of the Rebellion.

The following, in a pecuniary point of view, was even more valuable:

TREASURY DEPARTMENT, SECOND AUDITOR'S OFFICE,
August 15th, 1870.

This is to certify that the accounts of Major John M. Pomeroy, late Additional Paymaster, U. S. A., having been finally adjusted in this office and confirmed by the Second Comptroller, show no indebtedness on his part to the United States.

E. B. FRENCH, *Auditor.*

Many of the Paymasters, probably a majority, were short in their accounts, some a greater and others a less sum. Some of the Paymasters whose ability and integrity were unquestioned, found themselves short several thousand dollars, which they could not account for or explain, but which they were obliged to pay into the Treasury. The place was a very difficult and dangerous one to fill. The rolls were made by volunteer officers who were suddenly thrown into the service, and they were often inaccurate and in bad condition, while the disbursements were enormous and in small sums. Added to this the danger from thieves and rebels made the position a very hazardous one, and it is a wonder that the work was generally so accurately done. At the final settlement of the accounts of Major Pomeroy the United States was found to be indebted to him thirty-two dollars which was an unusual outcome.

The first sheets of this work were given to the compositor early in 1879, and were worked along very leisurely as time and inclination suited until August of that year, when the author had a spell of sickness which left him in enfeebled health for several months, during which time the work was suspended. It is now completed in the last days of April, 1880. The history, I hope, will be useful to those who may continue it in the present and future generations. But little has been said of the living of the generation of which the writer is a member, but full justice can be done to them by those who are now living.

The author has been careful not to blow his own horn, but as it happens several articles of a complimentary and personal nature are appearing in the papers as we are writing these final lines, I will add some of them and thus close.

From the *Public Opinion*, Chambersburg, Pa.:

As will be seen by the communication of "A Republican" in another column, the editor of orr venerable and esteemed contemporary, the *Repository*, is advanced as a candidate for the Legislature. Major Pomeroy represented this county in the Legislature a good many years ago, and there are a great many of our leading citizens of both parties who think that he combines all the elements necessary for a representative at the present time. He is well and favorably known throughout the State, and in the matter of the payment of the border claims, would exert an influence possessed by few others our county might send to the Legislature.

———

Communication from *Public Opinion:*

In my humble opinion, side by side, if not superior, to the Presidential, is the interest and importance that surrounds the office of members of the Legislature. Never in the history of State politics was this office of greater importance to the party. A United States Senator is to be chosen, a redistricting of the State, and an entire revision of the revenue laws of the State will compose some of the important work to be done. And last, and of much interest to the people of the county, is the Border Raid Bill which should be pushed with redoubled energy. These claims were never in better shape (thanks to

our present Assemblymen) than at present, and in making selections for this office, we should secure gentlemen who are willing not only to vote but to fight these claims to a final adjustment; and to this end I suggest the name of Major John M. Pomeroy, editor of *Franklin Repository*, as a very suitable candidate for this office. The Major is peculiarly fitted for a successful legislator. His acquaintance with the public men of the State is second to no gentleman in the county. His legislative experience, having been a member of former Legislatures, his successful career as editor by which he has become acquainted with the people of the county, and through which he has learned the feelings and wishes of the whole people; his advocacy of the Border Raid Bill at all times and on every occasion; his natural abilities; his unimpeachable character as a gentleman; his sound Republicanism —combine to make him a candidate the whole party could cheerfully support; and if nominated and elected, will not only be an honor to himself but the constituency he represents.

From the *Franklin Repository :*

SOMETHING PERSONAL.—The Lebanon *Courier* says: "The Republicans of Franklin county are talking of running Major John M. Pomeroy for the Legislature. He would be an ornament to that body, and is the kind of man the people will send to the Legislature if they are as anxious for good representatives as they claim to be."

As this matter has got into the papers, and is being generally commented upon, without any agency of mine, it may be proper to say that after mature reflection, I have concluded to be a candidate, and will be glad if my friends will relieve me of the necessity of making any general canvass of the county for the nomination. This practice, of recent origin, would be more honored in the breach than the observance. My aversion to electioneering caused me long to hesitate about being a candidate when pressed by many personal friends to enter the list, who are partial enough to think that I can be useful in aiding the important local interests they will have in the next Legislature. Even if I had an unwillingness, which I have not, to return to a position to which the Whigs of this county twice elected me, the wishes of many valued friends is conclusive as to my course now. I am obliged to my brethren of the press throughout the State for their too favorable

notices, and I will be grateful to my friends in the county for their support at the approaching Convention

J. M. P.

From the *Juniata Tribune:*

This week's *Franklin Repository* gives the announcement that its able editor, John M. Pomeroy, will be a candidate for Legislative honors in Franklin County. As that county has a habit of sending Republican members to the Legislature, we know of no one in the opposition who is better qualified to go, or who will give better satisfaction when he gets there. He ought to have no opposition for nomination.

From the Philadelphia *Times:*

Major John M. Pomeroy, editor of the Chambersburg *Repository*, has formally assented to the use of his name as a Republican candidate for the Legislature, and his nomination and election are reasonably assured. He represented Franklin in the House more than a generation ago. In 1845 he was first nominated by the Whigs and figured in the campaign as "the boy Pomeroy," but he defeated one of the ablest Democrats of the county by a decided majority and was re-elected in 1846. He is on his native heath in the Green Spot, and his known influence with the prominent men of his party throughout the State make his election to the House specially important to the local interests of the border counties.

We may add that we had no desire to return to a place we occupied thirty-five years ago, when we had barely attained our majority, and which was a more honorable position then than now, but many of our friends thought that on account of our previous experience, and extensive acquaintance, we might possibly aid them in securing the payment of their War Claims. There are other important questions to come before the next Legislature that may render it interesting. I am indifferent about it, and if it comes without any effort on my part, I will accept it, if not will be equally content.

ERRATA.

Page 37, last line—for appreciate read approach.

Page 49, on 17th line from top—read open for upper.

Page 51, on 14th line from top—read won for wore.

Page 82, on 4th line from foot—omit Samuel, and Samuel Davidson on the line below should have been reported dec'd.

Page 97, on 5th line from top—read than for that, and on same page, 5th line from foot, read divest for divert.

SD - #0129 - 200223 - C0 - 229/152/11 - PB - 9781334074981 - Gloss Lamination